T0158944

MARV RUBINSTEIN'S BOOKS

Pardon! An unashamed peddler since the age of 10.

Still, I know you'll enjoy my other books.

TO THE RAMPARTS!

Religion vs. Science—the Battle

OLD AGE AIN'T FOR WIMPS

Comedic Laments from an Aging Sage

WOMANIZER

"Knowing" Wonderful Women

NET-WIT.COM

A Smorgasbord of Internet Humor

NOW YOU'RE COOKIN'—WITH TEA

(with Chie Rubinstein)

Using Tea as an Ingredient in Cooking

FEATHER IN MY YARMULKE

Fond Memories of an Infant Israel

COMPENDIUM OF AMERICAN ENGLISH

A Guide to the Idiosyncrasies of American English

AVAILABLE FROM AMAZON, BARNES & NOBLE, ETC.

LIFE OF A
SALESMAN

ADVICE AND DIVERSIONS

MARVIN RUBINSTEIN

iUniverse LLC
Bloomington

LIFE OF A SALESMAN
ADVICE AND DIVERSIONS

Copyright © 2013 Marvin Rubinstein.

All rights reserved. No part of this book may be used or reproduced by any means, graphic, electronic, or mechanical, including photocopying, recording, taping or by any information storage retrieval system without the written permission of the publisher except in the case of brief quotations embodied in critical articles and reviews.

iUniverse books may be ordered through booksellers or by contacting:

iUniverse
1663 Liberty Drive
Bloomington, IN 47403
www.iuniverse.com
1-800-Authors (1-800-288-4677)

Because of the dynamic nature of the Internet, any web addresses or links contained in this book may have changed since publication and may no longer be valid. The views expressed in this work are solely those of the author and do not necessarily reflect the views of the publisher, and the publisher hereby disclaims any responsibility for them.

Any people depicted in stock imagery provided by Thinkstock are models, and such images are being used for illustrative purposes only.

Certain stock imagery © Thinkstock.

ISBN: 978-1-4917-0327-4 (sc)
ISBN: 978-1-4917-0326-7 (hc)
ISBN: 978-1-4917-0325-0 (e)

Library of Congress Control Number: 2013914587

Printed in the United States of America.

iUniverse rev. date: 08/30/2013

DEDICATION

I have run out of family and friends to whom I would normally dedicate this book. My wife Chie; my children Jonathan, Jay and Sari; my grandchildren David, Joanne and Clementine are all solidly in my heart but have already received book dedications. My wife suggests that I dedicate the book to our dog Chibi, but to me, that is too whimsical.

So, let me make a sentimental choice. I dedicate this book to Arthur Miller, who departed this life in 2005, but whose play *Death of a Salesman* pulled (and still pulls) the emotional heartstrings of millions of Americans, and particularly those of salesmen all over the world.

EPIGRAPH

"You don't understand: Willy was a salesman and for a salesman, there is no rock bottom to the life. He don't put a bolt to a nut, he don't tell you the law or give you medicine. He's a man out there in the blue, riding on a smile and a shoeshine. And when they start not smiling back, that's an earthquake. And then you get yourself a couple of spots on your hat, and you're finished. Nobody dast blame this man. A salesman has got to dream boy." [*]

---

[*]   *Death of A Salesman* by Arthur Miller

TABLE OF CONTENTS

PROLOGUE

The scene. A private room in a restaurant in Bangkok, Thailand. The time: quite a few years ago. This is not an ordinary restaurant. It was called the "Siam No-Hands Restaurant," and what makes it distinctive is that you are not allowed to use your hands in eating or drinking while you are there. Proper Thai matrons call it the "Disabled Man's Restaurant."

The cast of characters: an American international salesman and two Thai business associates who are his hosts for the evening. Also present are three attractive Thai ladies, whom each of the guests had selected from a lineup at the entrance. The young ladies are native Thais, with thick black hair and dark eyes. Though young, each has been thoroughly schooled in the ways of keeping a man happy.

A waiter brings in the menus, which feature Chinese food, and the pretty ladies assist in suggesting the tastiest dishes. Just how does one dine without the use of one's hands? Very simple. Each of the young ladies is assigned the task of feeding her particular customer. She feeds you using fork or chopsticks and tilting your glass upwards so you can drink water or wine or whatever. You can still use your hands, but not for eating. Hugging is OK. Or patting an attractive shoulder or a well-rounded derriere, but don't you dare touch a fork or spoon, the traditional culinary tools in Thailand. [Strange to say, in Thailand, chopsticks are only standard in Chinese restaurants.] Of course, conversation, teasing, flirtation and laughter are not only allowed but encouraged. As ordered by the hosts, once the main course had been consumed, another young lady enters the private dining room, proceeding slowly to divest herself of clothes and dancing seductively in the nude. She then sits herself down on the lap of the American guest and insists on feeding him his dessert.

The rules of the game clearly forbid any intense sexual activity. This is intended to be a restaurant with entertainment, not a brothel. If so desired, some of the young ladies may be available after hours by private arrangement, but that is strictly up to them and not part of the restaurant scene.

For one who has not previously spent much time in the Far East and does not know Bangkok, all of this is new and exciting and titillating. Definitely something to write home to one's friends about. Needless to say, such entertainment is s.o.p. for many cities in the Far East. And it is one of the possible fringe benefits in the "Life of a Salesman."

DAD

My father was a salesman. One of the old kind who went from door to door. When he was young, he followed the carnival trail, hawking balloons and pennants and stuffed dolls. In the 1920s, he sold sewing machines for Mr. Singer, when they were the newest and hottest sales item in town. He sold life insurance when people were not used to the idea, when they superstitiously feared that having a life insurance policy was a sure way to tempt the fates and bring on an early death. For most of the later years of his life, when I was in my teens, he sold blankets, sheets, pillowcases and household furnishings from door to door. Everything was sold on a dollar-down-and-a-dollar-whenever-they-catch-you basis.

Dad was a familiar figure in the poorer parts of town, pulling his bundle of samples out of his Model T Ford and spreading them out for the ladies to see. He mimicked an Irish brogue for the shanty or lace curtain Irish ladies, and he offered a simple English mixed with the "soul talk" of the time in the local black (now called African American) neighborhoods. Incidentally, his talent for mimicry seems to have skipped a generation. Neither I nor my siblings are good at it, but my daughter Sari is a whiz. Dad worked from early morning to early evening in summer sweat and in the blustery winter cold of Rochester, New York. He worked his ass off.

He labored hard and long to ensure his family a livelihood, but mostly he worked to see that his two sons received a college education and became professionals—not peddlers like him. Both my brother and I became professionals. He earned a Bachelor of Arts, wanting to become a teacher. But the 1929 depression decided otherwise, and he ended up working for New York State, heading up an Unemployment Insurance Office. I hold two degrees—a B.S. in Chemistry and a J.Dr. in Law. You may call me Dr. Rubinstein. But blood is thicker than water. Twenty years back, I retired as Chairman of the Board and owner of a small but prosperous engineering firm with worldwide offices and representation. When we first developed our products, I used my skills in chemistry. From time to time, when we needed a business contract or a dunning letter, I used my skills in law. However, the success of the company depended, not on building a better mousetrap, but on selling it.

It wasn't long before my partner found himself in charge of the factory, while I was out beating the bushes to market our products, first in the Northeast, then in the entire United States and eventually overseas. I had my two degrees, but the financial success of the company depended upon my sales ability, so I became a salesman. Of course, I call myself a "sales engineer." But basically, I'm a peddler. The doors I knock on are a lot fancier than those my father knocked on, but we both knocked on doors. And I make a hell of a lot more money and live more lavishly than Dad could ever have imagined. But I'm still a peddler. If that sounds self-deprecating, it is not so intended. Isaac Stern proudly calls himself a "fiddler." I am proud to be a peddler.

Some time back, I sold my business for millions of dollars. My father never lived to see the great financial success his son achieved, and I'm not sure if he would have been pleased or disappointed in how I turned out—rich but not a professional. As for me, I am a salesman and have never regretted it.

This book is about the life of a salesman. In truth, it will not deal with salesmen in candy stores or boutiques or Macy's. Nor will it deal with the salesman in a showroom, be it clothing or automobiles. These salesmen will have shared some of the experiences I shall discuss, but not most. This book is about the life of a salesman in the great outdoors, the one who goes from door to door or office to office or factory to factory. Much of my experience has been in selling overseas, practically all over the world, so I will write about that in some detail. However, I also spent years selling throughout the United States and Canada, and that will not be neglected.

This will not be an instruction book about the art of selling. It is instead an anecdotal reminiscence of one man who spent more than 50 years in national and international sales—the places he has been, the people he has met, the pleasures and perils of travel and the trials and tribulations of his chosen profession.

Without making any specific promises as to order or degree of importance, I would also like to convey some idea as to what the balance of this book will be about. There will be chapters or sections dealing with the following subjects: building a sales business, publicity and promotion on a piggy-bank budget. some observations on major U.S. cities, further observations on the major cities of the world, making the best of airline travel—some tips and suggestions, sightseeing on a fly-by-night schedule, local flora—wining and dining around the world, local fauna—meeting some lovely ladies internationally, doing business overseas, some so-called national characteristics and how to deal with them.

The above are provided to give the reader some idea as to where this book is going. To some degree, it will be a sales manual, but to a much larger degree it will be an adventure story about the funny and serious things that happened to me while living the Life of a Salesman.

Of course, there will be information on what the salesman must know and do in order to succeed. For those readers who themselves are salesmen, **these gems of sales wisdom will be highlighted in bold type.** But the sales approaches will be peripheral to the main outline of the story (or stories) I have to tell (and sell).

SALESMAN/SALESWOMAN

Perhaps one point should be made early in this book. Whenever I use the term "salesman," I do not intend to exclude the ladies. There are many wonderful and energetic young women out in the field. And they don't sell cosmetics only. My firm had very successfully used saleswomen to sell engineering products. I know of one international saleswoman who sold oil-drilling and oil-processing equipment, and spent time competing with males in such places as Saudi Arabia. In recent years, traveling saleswomen have become a familiar sight at the airports and factories of America. And, not strange to say, the lifestyle and mores and morals of the traveling saleswoman and the traveling salesmen are not dissimilar.

Why do I not use the term "salesperson"? Frankly, because I do not like the word. It seems turgid and lacks the snap of the word "salesman." If Arthur Miller's famous play had been entitled *Death of a Salesperson*, it would probably still have succeeded, but I feel certain that success would have taken longer. I feel no disrespect for the liberated and enlightened women of the world. I have always favored equal pay for equal work; promotion based on ability rather than sex; nurseries in factories to help working mothers and anything else which gives women a fair break in a not overly just world. But I also have a soft spot for properly spoken and written English. To my mind, muddying up the language (with a few exceptions) does nothing to improve the lot of women and only succeeds in . . . well, muddying up the language. One further point. While I have noted that saleswomen on the road are rapidly becoming part of the selling scene, up to now the vast majority of people in this field have been men. My experiences on the road, and those of my colleagues, have been the experiences of men—salesmen. Consequently, I am calling this book **Life of a Salesman**. It shouldn't be too long before some bright, active woman describes her experiences in a book called *Life of a Saleswoman.*" More power to her.

IN THE BEGINNING

Bangkok, Rio, London, Paris, Tel-Aviv, Tokyo—the names come trippingly off my tongue. A niece of mine, listening to my conversation, once accused me of being a "place dropper." She was right. As a salesman for more than 60 years, I have been marketing products in well over 75 different countries. This includes every industrial country in the world except Russia. At the start of this period, when I spent most of my time, traveling in the U.S., I peddled our products in 48 of the 50 States. If you include one plane stop at an Alaskan airport—where I made one successful phone call—it might add up to 49 States. With apologies to Bill Clinton, I missed Arkansas.

I vaguely remember a 1975 movie entitled "The Man who would be King." Two British soldiers of fortune (played by Sean Connery and Michael Cain) get trapped in a snow slide in the mountains of Northern India. Believing that they have had it, they sit before a small fire and reminisce. One of them comments that, even if this were the end, it had all been worthwhile. "Oh, the things we have seen, and the places we have been."

Empathizing with these old soldiers, I too have seen and been. I have spent time in almost all the major cities of the world; know many of their mean streets and grand boulevards; have dined or nibbled in their restaurants and bistros and food stalls; have been entertained by their women; seen their sights and smelled their smells.

I have worked with businessmen and engineers at almost all the major world airlines; at air force bases and naval maintenance facilities; at hundreds of international industrial firms and many smaller ones.

Oh, the things I have seen and places I have been.

This, however, is a far cry from where it all began. I suppose that I could tell you that, at the age of five or six or seven, I was already trading stamps or baseball cards or something with the other kids in my neighborhood. That is possible, but frankly my memory does not provide such details. My first genuine sales efforts started about the age of 12 or 13 when I read an ad in the Rochester, NY Democrat & Chronicle for sales boys to peddle magazines door to door. This was my first legitimate selling job. I jumped at the opportunity to make some spending money over and above the meager allowance that my family's means allowed. It sounded like an easy way to make a buck.

Easy? Ha! Neighbors were a little more willing to answer the door in those years than they are today, but not necessarily more willing to buy magazines—particularly from a stammering youth, shy and unseasoned in his chosen trade. Magazine orders were few and far between.

It did not take me long to discover that one of the basic problems was shyness on my part. Friends who know me today would never believe it, but I was a timid boy, an introvert. Did I march quickly up to each house and briskly knock at the door? No. Picture a scared youngster hesitating between stops, particularly if the last encounter had been an unfriendly one. When I reached the door, I paused for at least another minute before knocking or ringing the bell, uncertain to the very end as to whether I had the courage to proceed.

All these hesitations meant that the number of calls I was able to make in the limited time I had available between school hours and homework were minimal. I had yet to learn what every good salesman knows, that the number of calls you make per hour or per day is a critical element in the salesman's equation for success. **Selling**

is after all a numbers game. All else being equal, there is a straight-line relationship between the number of contacts, the number of sales calls made and the number of sales made. The percentages of successful sales as compared to calls may be small, but there is a strong correlation.

Compounding this dilatory shyness was my belief at that age, that an answer of "no" meant no. It was many years before I realized that **a "no" could mean "maybe" or even occasionally "yes"**—an ignorance which unfortunately was to cause me fateful embarrassment during my teenage courting years. When the lady at the door answered, "I don't think we are interested," which to a seasoned salesman means "maybe," I thanked her and promptly left. What I should have done was to puff up the advantages of the wonderful products I was selling, these magazines and journals which would bring joy and adventure into her life and entertainment and education to the whole family. And, of course, such a presentation had to be given with deep sincerity. As one comedian (I believe it was George Burns) once observed, "Sincerity is the key. If you can fake that, you have it made."

Well, we live and learn. Experience is costly and my first efforts at being a salesman were a dismal failure. That job lasted less than two months before I gave up, retreating to my books and my friends. But I still needed additional spending money. Where to find it? My father stepped in at this point and made a suggestion from his early years, namely that I try to sell balloons at periodic holiday parades taking place in my city. This seemed a frightening prospect. Facing the crowds and multitudes at a parade was considerably more terrifying than facing an individual prospective magazine purchaser at the door. The result was that, while I eventually tried this, a year passed before I got up enough courage. Necessity is after all the mother of invention.

Lo and behold, selling balloons at a parade was far easier than peddling magazines door to door. You are dealing with people in a festive mood and with fathers and mothers who want to please little Joe or Sally. Selling balloons at a parade did not take much convincing, since the number of available purchasers was relatively huge as compared to the number of sales people around. All that was needed was a loud and energetic voice letting everyone within earshot know that you were there and what you had to peddle. It was here that I learned **two additional essential elements in peddling: Pick a product to sell which has a relatively large number of potential customers. Then, make sure that you promote it so that everyone knows where to make his purchase.**

Did I mention a "festive air"? It is true. When people are happy, on a vacation, on a day off from work, taking the children out for fun, there is something about the spirit which develops and which loosens the purse strings. This concept was reinforced many years later. I was then living in Carmel, California, an extremely beautiful little town and a vacation Mecca for loads of tourists. I had a conversation with a French lady who owned a linen shop there. She told me that the shop in Carmel did so much better than one she had previously had in San Francisco, because the vacation spirit separated the tourists from their money much more rapidly.

This is why so many important sales are really concluded on a golf course or over a three-martini lunch. I made what for me at that time was a lot of money selling balloons at parades and continued to do this for two or three years. There were only two strong negatives. First, there were not enough parades. The possible number of events where I could make a buck were limited in Rochester, New York. Had I known of the approximate "parade-a-week" potential in a place like New York City, I would have salivated at the thought. Second, inclement weather was always a downer. The first problem taught me another selling principle: **Go where the opportunities are. Don't try selling ice to the Eskimos**. The weather problem I still have not solved.

The concept of not trying to sell ice or even refrigerators to the Eskimos seems transparently valid, but is not always so. In sales work, a little imagination goes a long way. A typical peddler story tells of two salesmen sent to darkest Africa many years ago to explore the market for shoes. The first wired his company: "No sales potential here. Nobody wears shoes." The second wired his firm: "Tremendous sales possibilities here. Nobody wears shoes yet." ("A salesman has got to dream.") Africa has come a long way since then, but there remain parts of Africa, Asia or South America where this story still has force.

Speaking of shoes, in addition to the festive type of sales made at parades and gatherings, during my high school years and during Summer vacations in my early college years, there were two other sales jobs worthy of note-worthy, that is, on a small scale. The first was the only job in my life where I ever got fired. It still rankles, and I have always suspected that the excuse for the discharge was simply an excuse, due to the fact that the boss had too many salesmen on the floor. This job involved Saturday work selling women's shoes at a shoe store. In the trade, the occupation is known as being a "shoe dog" and, strange to say, many men spend their lives on their knees being shoe dogs. My stay in the business was much more limited— about two months. Then, on a critical day, while attempting to lace a lady's boot, a slightly sharp corner of the lace's aglet caught the lady's stocking and created a run. I apologized profusely, but she complained to the manager. He fired me on the spot.

Was I a careless salesman or was the sharp spot on the aglet a product defect? I guess I shall never know, but it taught me some other lessons about the vicissitudes of selling. **The first was that the product being sold may itself trip you up. Watch out for minor defects. The second lesson was that, when business is dull, the least productive salesman or the one who was last hired is the first to go,** often with the rationale that you did something wrong. Still, this shoe dog job had its peripheral benefits. It was a socially acceptable way of looking up women's skirts. And, believe it or not, some wore nothing else underneath. I am convinced deliberately so. A new and exciting experience for a young sprout.

One summer, during my early college years, I spent a three-month stint selling women's dresses at a dress shop whose clientele were mostly mature Italian or Latino ladies. This means that the sizes were large and the color in those days could be anything as long as it was black. If you wondered how a teenager got a job of this type, the answer is "connections." My sister owned the dress shop.

It was a pleasant sales job involving interaction between the potential customers and me—a more lengthy and somewhat more personal interaction than the quick one-two-three sale of balloons. And it gave me more confidence than being down on my knees selling shoes. **I learned the necessity of developing a salesman's patter, some amiable conversation on non-business matters to establish rapport or bonding between the seller and the sellee. Years later, I realized that a collection of jokes and anecdotes was possibly a *sine qua non* for keeping the potential customer's attention.**

I retain one vivid memory of that job. My sister was a lovely person, but inclined to be bossy. (She continued working as a saleslady in a shop until the age of 84.) One day, while I was waiting on an oversized customer for an extended period of time, my sister showed lack of confidence in me by rushing over to be of additional service. The customer turned to her and very tartly commented, "Your help is not needed. This young man is taking very good care of me." I sold the lady two dresses, and both the comment and the sale helped build selling confidence for the future.

The experience of selling balloons at parades proved valuable when I moved on to Cornell University, where I definitely needed extra spending money over and above the costs covered by my scholarships and very limited aid from home. I quickly discovered that, in an area called College Town, there was a Student Cooperative which specialized in providing goods and services to the student body. One set of items they marketed were pennants, buttons, pins, flags, balloons and a variety of other festive items for sale at college sports events—particularly at football games, the big rah-rah-rah events of the college year. This Student Co-op was always looking for impoverished students to get out with the crowd carrying a display-board of products saleable to a boisterous group of football or other sports enthusiasts. A friend of mine, Stan, and I decided to join these youthful hucksters. There were good days and bad days as far as sales were concerned, but in general we did well financially. The few coins I earned then would seem picayune today but, at the time, they made the difference between my living "decently" and barely making ends meet.

Stan and I shortly discovered that the Co-op reserved sales management positions for those who sold the largest amounts in a given season. We talked about this, and arranged a minor conspiracy. Both of us had fairly respectable sales but, if one would shift half of his sales to the other, the results for the "superior" salesman might be substantial enough to create a management position the following term or year. And, since the sales manager got a percentage on everything sold, this could nicely be shared between Stan and me.

On paper, the scheme worked well. I still believe that my sales figures were higher than that of any other student out selling similar products. However, this led me to learn about **another significant fact which every salesman should know. It is not always what you know or how well you sell that counts; it is frequently "whom you know" that makes the big difference.** The cousin of the general manager of the sales cooperative got the sales management position for the coming year.

It is not my intention to indicate that selling was the main force in my life during my early years. Frankly, it was not. I was too busy with studies and numerous extra-curricular activities and friends and chess and family events to be highly involved in sales.

During my college years, since I was a Chemical Engineering student, the intensity of work was such that it left you little extra time. What time I did have left was divided between drinking beer with comrades or playing bridge with friends, starting minor courtships (another variety of salesmanship) and trying to earn some extra money whatever way I could. This involved washing dishes and pots and pans in a restaurant; correcting math papers for a professor; feeding regulated amounts of chemicals into containers at the hydroponics department of the School of Agriculture; etc. The selling of pennants and buttons was just a small part of this.

However, while the urge to be a salesman was not an overpowering element in my early life, it always lurked in the background. I was not out looking for it, but whenever an opportunity to sell at a profit came up, my motto was *"carpe diem."* I seized the opportunity. My knowledge and imagination as to where these opportunities lay were still very limited and, as noted, the time for seizing them was even more limited, but an early imprint on my psyche and experience told me that sales was a profitable area and, if you like dealing with people, it could be pleasant and fun as well.

So, on to bigger and better opportunities.

THE BIG APPLE

As a child, I visited relatives in New York City on several occasions, but my only memories involve the insides of railroad apartments and, more important, the inside of a candy store that an uncle of mine had in the Bronx. It was not until my 19th year that I really visited New York City and saw it through the eyes of at least a semi-adult. I arrived at Grand Central Station in the early evening and was picked up by my brother who was living in New York City at that time. As a sort of quick introduction to the City before we went to his apartment, he drove me around central Manhattan and Times Square. Wild eyed and exhilarated, staring raptly at the crowds, the lights and the sounds, I kept saying, "This is for me." My mind was made up then and there that someday I would come and live in this magnificent and dynamic city, what O. Henry called "Baghdad on the Subway."

Over the years, my attitude towards New York has undergone many changes, but I still remain wide-eyed about the place. One brief anecdote sums up the feelings of those of us aware enough to face facts but still wildly in love with this most exciting and fascinating hulk of a metropolis.

A friend of mine, an elderly gentleman of great charm, resided in a very small town in central Virginia where, among other things, he raised pedigreed cattle. My friend could take New York or leave it, but he did pay us a visit about once a year, principally to see his son who lived and worked in Manhattan. On his last trip, his son told him: "Dad, New York City is impossible. It is dirty. The air isn't fit to breathe. Both automobile and pedestrian traffic are the worst. New Yorkers are unbelievably rude. Life here is a constant hassle. Worse yet, New York has become more and more expensive. And, as I'm sure you've heard, the City can be dangerous."

My friend listened and nodded. "Well, son," he asked, "When are you leaving?" "Leaving?" replied the son, "who said anything about leaving?"

It was not until 1945 that, at the age of 23, I kept the promise to myself to move to New York. My hometown, Rochester, New York had bored me. My primary job as a plating chemist had bored me. I was ready for the big time. And I had prearranged by mail and phone for a new job in the Big Apple. Surprise, surprise. It was a sales job. My employer was an electroplating chemicals supply house. My potential customers were plating shops, metal finishing shops and metal treating shops throughout the greater New York area.

Since I did not own an automobile at the time, all of my sales trips were made via subway, bus or train. In no time flat, I became an expert on how to get from A to B, or more likely from A to Z, on all of the elaborate New York City subway systems. Every evening, I would map out the customers I wanted to visit in a certain part of the city and, with a subway map in front of me, plan just how I was going to see all of them, using my travel time as efficiently as possible.

Subways were reasonably safe at that time (and are even more so today), and the only problem was making sure that you got off at the right stop and made the proper connection. It was—and still is—a fine high-speed system for getting around a complex city. The Paris Metro is much quieter, the one in Madrid much cleaner and the Washington, DC one more attractive but, noisy and dirty as it is, and occasionally dangerous, the New York subway system does what it was intended to do, i.e. speed people over substantial distances from home to work or any other place you might desire.

This need to visit plating shops throughout all of greater New York using public transportation certainly honed **two necessary elements**

in the skill of selling. The first was dividing up your sales territory into small, easily handled areas so that you could maximize the number of calls you would be able to make in a day. The second was establishing the most effective and efficient means of getting to and between calls. Both of these skills were to stand me in good stead throughout the rest of my sales career.

Although my new sales job was excellent in establishing a learning curve, it was far less effective in making a living. Early on, it seemed to me that I was a superb salesman. I had no problems whatsoever selling tons of copper carbonate, nickel sulfate, chromic acid, caustic soda, potassium cyanide and all the other materials generally used in the electroplating field. Unfortunately, **there are two sides to every sales picture, namely supply and demand.** Demand was definitely there, and I was able to write up numerous orders, certainly sufficient to support myself in a reasonable lifestyle. However, supply was not available.

This job was during World War II, and there were substantial shortages in industrial materials, particularly in industrial chemicals. My boss wanted me to sell those limited chemicals which he had available in stock. My potential customers wanted to buy everything else but. The end result was cataclysmic. The job paid a small base salary, but earnings were intended to depend primarily on a percentage of sales made. The term "sales made" really meant "sales shipped and paid for." Ergo, Q.E.D., since the needed supply of chemicals for which I had orders were not available, my commissions were close to zero.

After about four months, the need to eat forced me to give up this wonderful sales job and return to work as a plating chemist with a company manufacturing photograph record masters and stampers. My commercial sales career in New York was apparently in shambles.

I didn't at this time know that sales was my destiny, but I did learn one hard rule about the sales field. While my instincts told me that it could lead to great prosperity, my first real commercial industrial selling experience taught me that it was often catch-as catch-can. It was often feast or famine. **While in theory one could earn big bucks as a salesman, in practice, there were a large number of variables which could severely limit your income.** So for the time being at least, I took a nice secure industrial job which provided me a steady dependable income, so that I could eat and carry on a reasonable social life. Quite a few years were to pass before I became actively involved in commercial sales again.

POLITICAL SALES

I did, however, soon after this, take on what proved to be one of the most difficult selling jobs of my life. This was not a commercial job for income but a volunteer position which kept me busy evenings and weekends. I became involved in politics. In a small way, of course, but still it was politics.

The post-war years were turbulent political times. As a flaming young liberal, I could not find satisfaction in the positions of either the Republican party or the Democratic party. Consequently, when Franklin D. Roosevelt dropped Henry Wallace as a Vice-Presidential candidate for his next term and substituted Harry S, Truman instead, and when Wallace decided to run independently for President, I felt that here was a place in the political spectrum where I could find people whose political point of view was compatible with mine. I became very active in the Wallace for President movement.

In retrospect, I might add that I now believe I took the wrong path. Today, I firmly believe that Harry S. Truman was one of the best Presidents that the United States has ever had, and that Henry Wallace's subsequent positions on a number of issues were not well thought out. Be that as it may, this is hindsight and, to quote Harry, "Did I ever tell you that any schoolboy's hindsight is worth all the President's foresight?"

Activity in the Henry Wallace Presidential campaign involved going to many meetings, listening to and sometimes contributing to long discussions and taking part in a number of activities, so as to advise the general public how terrific your candidate (product) was. I occasionally spoke at street rallies, attended the Henry Wallace Nominating Convention as an Alternate and passed out flyers and promotional material on street corners and at rallies.

This in turn led me to writing promotional material. I put together numerous handbills for my local Henry Wallace Club and was an active contributing editor to our local newsletter. What has this got to do with selling? Plenty. **It is one thing to build a better mouse trap, but until you have advised the general public, spread the good word, delivered the message that your mousetrap is better and you have it readily available, you have not made a sale. This, in a small way was my introduction to Marketing—a very valuable and necessary introduction to selling**—a subject to be dealt with in more detail later in this book.

Work on the Wallace Campaign essentially lacked an active focus until such time as a political change took place in New York State. A third party, the American Labor Party, became an active advocate for the Wallace campaign and included his name in their party line on the ballot for the Presidency. Subsequently—and against my better judgment—the Wallace Campaign and the American Labor Party Campaign were merged in New York State. The Wallace Campaign newsletter I was editing at the time featured a banner headline "Merger Will Out." Guess who thought up that one.

In order to remain active in the campaign, I had to become a member of an A.L.P. Club, and the one closest to me on the upper East Side of Manhattan was one run by Vito Marcantonio—a spellbinding left-wing Congressman and an active leader in the American Labor Party. As a member of his local Club, I was given a more highly focused job to do, namely that of becoming a District Captain for the Club for a two-square-block area on the Upper East Side of Manhattan. The job involved getting to know virtually everyone who lived in that area; making periodic visits to their apartments in the early evening or weekends; trying to talk them into voting for Henry Wallace and, in a subsequent campaign, for Vito Marcantonio for Congress. [Not too dissimilar to the practices in the Barack Obama campaigns, except that we lacked the convenience of electronic communication.]

This was my first real job (non-paid) at selling intangibles (from the Latin *tangere*, meaning "to touch"). For the uninitiated, tangible sales can involve anything that you can see, feel or smell, e.g. fruits, vegetables, clothes, refrigerators, automobiles, etc. Intangible sales include such items as life insurance and stocks and bonds. There are numerous other intangibles being sold to the public on a regular basis, e.g. true religion and, in my case, political candidates. Sometimes the last two are confused.

As testified to by the multimillion-dollar campaigns carried out by today's Senators, Congressmen, Governors and (most of all) Presidential candidates, these candidates must be packaged and sold pretty much in the same way that you sell a bar of soap. If all of this sounds rather cynical and lacking glamour and feeling, it is regrettable, but it is nevertheless true. I had become involved in intangible sales—the selling of Henry Wallace and Vito Marcantonio. And, believe me, I was doing a damned good job at it.

Henry Wallace turned out to be a flash in the pan and retired to raising chickens in Upstate New York. Vito Marcantonio remained a gadfly Congressman, constantly irritating both Republicans and Democrats until they succeeded in ganging up on him a number of years later. He had previously run on both the Democratic and American Labor Party tickets until the State Democratic Committee changed the rules so that, even if he won the Democratic primary, he could not run as a Democrat without the approval of the Committee. All of this happened several years later. Shortly after his ouster, Marcantonio died of a heart attack while walking across City Hall Park.

The ultimate political fate of Vito Marcantonio was similar to those at that political period of our history who were accused of being Communists and failed to recant. I knew the man fairly well, and frankly doubt if he were a card-carrying Communist, though he did share some of their ideas, as do many other Americans. He was in fact a populist and a bit of a rabble-rouser. However, as a Congressman, he was enough of an irritant to the power structure to help prevent some of the worst conservative legislation being considered. But that is history.

While working as a District Captain during a Marcantonio campaign, I was assigned a two-square-block area in the East 70s between First and Second Avenues. This neighborhood has now been gentrified, with rents raised accordingly but, at that time, it was a lower middle-class neighborhood populated by a diverse group of people with a substantial number of Italians and Eastern Europeans—some immigrants and some second generation. In general, they were people of socially conservative backgrounds who could only be prompted to voting for a liberal candidate if they became convinced that it was good for their pocketbooks. Many of them, but not all, had high school educations at best and were easily moved by propaganda— mine or the other side's—in the newspapers or over the radio. I could see very quickly that organizing these two square blocks and bringing in a sizable majority vote for Vito Marcantonio was going to be a difficult selling job.

To begin with, my time was limited. I had a regular job from 9 to 5, and the only time I could ring doorbells in the neighborhood was in the early evening on weekdays and part of the day on Saturday. Not too early in the evening, please, since people did not like being disturbed while eating their suppers. (The term "dinner" had not yet become popularized.) Nor did most of them like your coming too late. I soon found that 7:30 to 9:30 p.m. was the best time, with a few possible individuals who could tolerate a later hour. This business of timing your visits was again a piece of selling knowledge which I was able to put to good use in later years in industrial sales.

If a salesman likes to get in a full day of selling, and his watch shows 4:30 p.m., it pays to have accumulated a list of small businesses where the owner works late and does not mind receiving a sales call after 5:00 p. m. or sometimes even after 7:00 p.m.

As an example, I remember several years back visiting a small industrial firm in Philadelphia about 6:30 p.m. The owner was on my sales rep's special "late list." We made a leisurely sales pitch for nearly an hour, including some amiable chatter and a couple of salesmen's stories. The owner seemed in no hurry for us to leave. About 7:30 p.m., I consulted my watch and asked the customer, "Do you always work this late?" "Usually until about 9:00 p.m.," he replied. "And what time do you start in the morning?" I asked. "Oh, about eight." I was perplexed, so l asked, "Doesn't your wife object?" There was a pause. The customer then looked me straight in the eye. "Marv," he said, "behind every successful businessman is a wife who's a bitch." [Don't quote me on this. That is what the man said.]

Back to my political sales days (or evenings). I too had a late list. Some of these were political buffs (on both sides of the spectrum) who enjoyed lengthy discussions on the issues. These needed to be kept for last; otherwise, they would consume your whole evening on a single call. And then there were some nice young ladies who enjoyed company. More on that subject later.

One problem with my district was that many of the residents did not have their names on the downstairs bell or, in some cases even on the mailboxes. They had emigrated from countries where it was much safer to remain anonymous. Again, a lesson I learned about selling. **If you are going to use a list of any sort for a mailing or telephone campaign, it is much, much better to have the names of the individuals available than to use terms such as "Department Head" or "Occupant."** It became apparent to me early on that I needed to organize the area in such a way that I would know the names of virtually all of the residents and which apartments they occupied. To some degree, I already knew the names, since we had lists of registered voters in my assigned blocks, but I did not know on what floor and in which apartment they lived. And a large number of those buildings were (and some still are) five-floor walk-ups. **Another sales lesson: Selling can involve unexpectedly hard physical labor.**

So I decided to do my organizing first before doing my personal calling. A wise sales decision. I walked into the hallway of each building with my list of names and proceeded to enter into a notebook any apartment information that was available on either the bells or the mailboxes. In some cases, where almost no information was available downstairs, I walked or took an elevator to the top floor and made notes on any names on apartment doors as I descended. Some people who did not keep their names on their buzzers or mailboxes did so on their entrance doors. [A similar problem exists today, when you may have street addresses, but not E-mail addresses.] When I had finished gathering as much information as I could in this way, I then approached superintendents in order to fill in the remaining names. This was not always easy, since the superintendents were also frequently recent immigrants who were only doing the job for the price of a free apartment, and whose experience in their home countries had also made them suspicious of inquiring strangers. However, some of the superintendents were Marcantonio buffs, and that really helped.

I will not say that I developed a complete list of everybody in those two square blocks, but over a period of a month or so, I accumulated a reasonably accurate list of at least 90 percent of the residents. Now began the task of calling on them and giving them my political sales pitch.

BACK TO KNOCKING ON DOORS

Over ten years had passed since that shy young boy had been hesitant about knocking on a neighborhood door in order to peddle his magazines. Ten years had made many changes, but *plus ça change, plus ça reste la même chose.* Now we have a somewhat more aggressive but not totally secure young man again ready to knock on neighborhood doors. One would think that the intervening years would have built enough confidence so that I could aggressively move ahead with my political selling job. Nay, not so. If I had been knocking on doors of people in my own age group, at my own social and economic level, in the ethnic family with which I was most familiar, things might have been a bit easier. However, in a sense, I was back to the age of 12. At that earlier time, it was the age discrepancy that had frightened me. How was a young boy of 12 to communicate the excellence of a product to a potential customer, a total stranger, who was usually a mature married man or woman?

By the time I started to do political canvassing, my age level was not too distant from that of the potential "customer," but I was more aware of other differences. Today, as a hard-boiled salesman of many years experience, I strongly feel that I now have no problems communicating with CEO's of large corporations; with owners of small businesses (often with only moderate educations); with engineers and chemists; with machinists, mechanics and maintenance men; and of course with their secretaries and receptionists. It no longer matters that many of them drink beer while I prefer wine. Nor am I fazed by the fact that they want to discuss baseball or basketball and the results of last night's game, while I would prefer to talk about books or the theatre or perhaps even politics. I needed to remain *au courant* enough on some of their interests so as to establish rapport with possible clients, but I am no longer faced with doubts or hesitations.

The truth is that young intellectual types with little daily contact with working class guys do not normally feel at ease under those circumstances. Even today, I find it difficult to accept the fact that the Archie Bunkers of this world often show more camaraderie with African-Americans or other minorities they deride than the do-gooders who spend time and energy being politically active on behalf of the underprivileged or those who work with their hands. Not that there's anything wrong with their contributions. It's just that the personal relations are often awkward.

With regular contact and experience over the years, however, one eventually eases up and realizes that people are people, and a good salesman soon learns how to communicate at just about every level. As to possible subjects of mutual interest, there is always politics, sex and (for some) religion. A good supply of jokes also helps.

Those three items take me back to a party I attended in Oklahoma about 35 years back. I was there representing my company, and was known to all as a very aggressive salesman for our product, the Selectron Process. More than that, at that time, I lived and breathed Selectron, Selectron, Selectron. Everyone at the party knew that and considered me Mr. Selectron. My hosts were a charming African-American couple, who had carefully invited those they considered most interesting among a group of engineers attending a conference on aircraft maintenance. Among the guests was an Ethiopian engineer representing Ethiopian Airlines. "Serge," I asked him, "please tell me something about Ethiopian politics." "Marv," he responded, "I will talk to you about anything except politics." This apparently was a dangerous subject for an Ethiopian at that time, and possibly even now. "Well," I said, "that's too bad. By avoiding politics, you are

eliminating one of the only four subjects in life worth discussing."
At that point, my host joined in, "Really, Marv, what are those four
subject?" I quickly replied, "sex, politics, religion and the Selectron
Process." **A *sine qua non* for selling success: You must be totally
involved with your product.** A little humor doesn't hurt, either.

But let us get back to the late 40s and early 50s, when I lacked my
present *savoir faire*. As previously mentioned, many of the people
on whose doors I was to knock were recent immigrants and spoke
limited English. A large percentage of them were blue-collar workers.
Since this was a mixed neighborhood, at the other end of the scale
were some educated and well-read, politically savvy individuals who
liked nothing better than to lock horns with someone of my political
philosophy. I didn't know this at the beginning, but reality dawned
on me very quickly, and again I was that 12-year old boy standing in
front of the door wasting seconds or minutes of precious time trying
to decide whether I had the courage to knock and enter. However, I
had promised to do a job, and personal pride indicated that—hesitant
or not—I had to do it.

In reality, it was not so bad. Most people were relatively nice to
deal with. If they were busy or having dinner, some would suggest
that you come back later or another day. If they disagreed with you
politically, most were polite about it. Only a few were vociferously
antagonistic. Political canvassing provides an excellent training area
for determining when a "no" means no or when (as in most cases) there
is a window of opportunity for making a "sale." Most people, while
they may lean to the left or right, are not so adamantly frozen in their
political attitudes that they are not open to some degree of change if a
good salesman can get to spend some time with them. Again, we were
reaching the sales platitude that a "no" could mean "maybe."

Of course, there were exceptions. A few doors were slammed in
my face, and a few people told me to "get the hell out of here" in a
tone which indicated I had better move quickly. And then there were
those interesting situations where Mama and Papa held politically
diverse points of view. I distinctly remember one lady who met me at

the door and, as soon as I mentioned Vito Marcantonio, put her finger to her lips. She whispered "I will meet you in the downstairs hallway." A few moments later, she joined me and begged me not to knock on her door again. She told me plaintively: "Don't worry about me. I will vote for Vito. But my husband is violently anti-communist and thinks that Marcantonio is one of them. If you insist upon coming to our apartment, you will only create a big battle between my husband and me. Please don't."

Any intelligent person, particularly any intelligent salesperson, listens carefully to appeals like that. It is not a salesman's job to make waves. A few ripples now and then may do no harm, but caution should prevail. I marked my records with one "yes" and one "no" for that apartment and never darkened that door again.

Many rudiments of selling can be learned while canvassing for political candidates. Get your facts straight. Perhaps more important, keep your facts simple. If you are to convince a large number of people, you must economize on time. Spend too much time in any one household, and you are limiting the number of possible "sales." Selling is a numbers game.

Lengthy and complicated explanations about your candidate or product will not sell. They will tend to bore the recipient rather than convince him. What I noted then and what I learned to deliver were equivalent to today's television sound bites—brief pointed comments on the advantages of my candidate and/or the disadvantages of the scurrilous opposition. Some people could be convinced quickly. Others were more hesitant. I had to learn—again for the sake of time and economy—which individuals might merit a second or third call, and which would probably be a waste of time.

Some people asked for more evidence. In more recent years, when I was in business, I would tell such possible clients that I will confer with my engineers and laboratory people and send them the data they requested. During my political canvassing, I had to do something similar, i.e. make a note as to what was needed and what I promised to deliver, Big rule: **If you promise to deliver additional data or facts,**

make sure you do so. Even in those days, I was aware of that cardinal rule and made it a point to see that I supplied written information on a variety of subjects when such information was requested by potential voters.

As in all selling, it is important to know your product and know it well. However, it is equally important not to spend a lot of time providing infinite details. Time is money. You provide enough information to whet the appetite of the possible voter or buyer, and then you go on your way, making a note in your notebook or on a file card as to when you should come back to complete the sale. This was a great learning experience for a salesman.

As mentioned earlier, there were of course special situations. One had to be particularly wary of people who could keep you in their apartment for hours, either because they needed company or for ulterior motives. There were those who for the most part agreed with my political point of view and welcomed the opportunity to discuss it at length. Many of these were nice people who had already been "sold." A good salesman quickly learns that, once the sale is made, get out of there quickly. You can talk yourself out of a sale just as easily as you talked someone into it. So one had to develop a polite technique for disengaging oneself from such individuals, pleasant though they might be.

On the opposite side of the political spectrum were those sly characters who never intended to vote for your candidate but enjoyed jousting. In a few cases, I suspected that this was a deliberate attempt to use up my time so that there would be fewer hours left for canvassing.

Let's talk about another possible fringe benefit in the selling game. There was another category of people I visited who should not be left out of this discussion. These were lonely young ladies, who welcomed an excuse for having a young man come into their apartments. Many of them were from outside New York. New York City provides wonderful grounds for aggressive young men and young women to meet one another at bars, art galleries, while walking a dog in the park, etc. However, for the shy immigrant to New York who does not own a dog, the process of meeting people can be very painful. The time for easy meeting of possible mates is during high school or college years. During those periods, there are ample opportunities to meet members of the opposite sex under informal surroundings. Once you have started to work, the opportunities are usually far less frequent. And this is particularly true if you have moved to another city and are of a shy or non-aggressive temperament.

I remember, many years later, interviewing a potential secretary who asked me "Mr. Rubinstein, do you have any unmarried men working here? Would I be able to meet unmarried men who visit your business?" When I advised her that, "Alas, no," she thanked me and told me that she was not interested in working for me; she was looking for a job where she could meet eligible young men. Smart girl.

Back to political canvassing. Some of the young women on whose doors I knocked were warm loving people. It was a happy hunting ground. Being a political canvasser gave you a socially acceptable reason for entering someone's apartment and gave the young ladies a socially acceptable reason for inviting you in. An informal conversation. A drink. A few stories and laughs and you had a new friend, usually one with whom you felt at least politically compatible.

On occasion, one thing led to another and these encounters in turn resulted in a few romances, of which I distinctly remember two. They had one peculiar shared characteristic. Each of them wept copiously after making love. Each for a totally different reason. One was a very strict Catholic girl from Texas (one quarter Cherokee Indian) who wept because she firmly believed that she was losing her place in heaven when she followed strong bodily and emotional instincts. This never stopped her from satisfying her biological and emotional needs, but she always cried afterward. The second was a young lady from the Midwest who had no sisters but seven brothers. These brothers had lovingly protected her through all the early years of her life until she came to New York. For some difficult to explain reason, she felt that the act of love was a betrayal of her seven brothers. And consequently she wept, and wept and wept. Many are the fascinating and heartwarming memories which remain after over 50 years in the life of a salesman.

The political selling years ended when Vito Marcantonio lost his job in Congress. I suppose I could have gone on following the ways of political selling, either on my own behalf or that of other candidates. However, when many of his former followers turned on Marcantonio and threw him out of office, it sort of took the heart out of me. To be totally honest, there were other factors. I was becoming very active in the business world. Numerous entrepreneurial ideas were perking in my mind, and I felt the need to give more time to these. However, I never have regretted the years I spent marketing political ideas, and **two important sales rules remain with me as a result of these experiences. First, if you want to sell well, you must believe in your product. Secondly, you must believe in yourself.**

WHAT IS A SALESMAN SELLING?

First, if you want to sell well, you must believe in your product. Secondly, you must believe in yourself. This is a good point to stop temporarily on my biographical sales history and discuss the subject of selling. When a salesman goes on the road, what is he selling? Soap, tractors, chemicals, bibles, cosmetics, photocopiers, etc? He may be selling any one or more of these, but he will never succeed unless he learns rule number one in the selling game: **The Salesman is Selling Himself.**

Before you can make an impact on any potential customer with any product whatsoever, you must find a way to get the potential buyer either to like you or be impressed by you—preferably both. This is true regardless of the nature of the product you may be selling. If you cannot sell yourself first, you cannot sell your product. People rarely buy from salesmen who turn them off. This is true not only in the industrial and commercial world, but even in cultural and aesthetic areas. To provide an example, let's briefly explore the field of art. Most artists do not become successful until after they have died. Their paintings may sell for millions of dollars, but they never lived to reap the benefits. For the most part, those artists who do sell at a great profit to themselves while still living are more than just capable or wonderful artists. They are also great salesmen.

Two names spring to mind: Pablo Picasso and Salvador Dali. Both of these gentlemen had two parallel careers: (1) providing superb art for the world and (2) selling it to the public in copious amounts. Let's face it. Picasso was a wonderful artist, but any visit to a Picasso collection will reveal that he did a number of mediocre paintings and sculptures as well. Good or bad, they all sold because Pablo Picasso projected an enormous personality to the world, one which made anyone who could afford it want to have a Picasso on his wall. Salvador Dali was in the eyes of the art world not so much a wonderful painter as a superb draftsman. He was also, I believe, somewhat of a con artist. Many of his works display weird or peculiar scenes which I believe were deliberately done that way to create a certain mystique. To sell these paintings, he projected a lifestyle so flamboyant as to be spectacular. And the constant promotion, the publicity and the ambiance he and his wife created about his work, made Dali's paintings sell like hotcakes, although at a somewhat higher price.

Both these gentlemen lived life to the hilt, traveled extensively, womanized (Picasso had three or four wives plus several long-term mistresses) and told the world in no uncertain terms, "If you buy one of our paintings, you will indicate to everyone who sees it that you are a superior person with fascinating tastes, not to mention the bankroll required to satisfy these tastes."

A more current well-known salesman/artist was Andy Warhol. Again, not a particularly great artist in the eyes of most of the artistic community, but one who unquestionably left his mark on modern art. But what a salesman! Before his death in 1987, his salesmanship cum artistic flare earned him a substantial fortune.

A living example is Mark Kostabi who presides over a Manhattan art production studio (or factory) in Soho known as Kostabi World. There, he and his assistants produce from 200 to 2,000 paintings a year, paintings which sell at $4,000. to $40,000. each. Kostabi is 53 years old, about as flamboyant as you can get, and with a flair for self-promotion. Mark Kostabi, by the way, is also a talented and self-touted musician. I mention him here because he recently was quoted as saying, "For me, marketing is a rest from painting, and painting is a rest from marketing." Get it? Incidentally, there is a documentary film about Kostabi. It is entitled *Con Artist.*

And, of course, the ability to sell oneself is not limited to the visual arts. In the field of music, Leonard Bernstein and Nigel Kennedy come to mind as highly talented self-promoters of the first order. The motto of all these artists is "Don't just paint something or play something; get out there and peddle it."

What I am saying is not unlike the simpler cry of Willy Loman in *Death of a Salesman.* To him, as a salesman, the most important thing was not to be just "liked," but to be "well liked." In other words, he had to sell himself.

NEW YORK INTERLUDE

After my initial sales debacle in New York, I settled down for several years in a variety of engineering jobs totally unrelated to sales. Not that the years were dull. My life has always been interesting and exciting, but this book is about selling, so I shall only dwell briefly on industrial and manufacturing activities. These included being Plant Manager in a firm manufacturing lipstick cases and military belt buckles; Foreman in a very busy commercial plating shop and Plating Chemist at a small phonograph record manufacturer.

Were there any sales activities? Well, I was a young man in my twenties in a city full of exciting young ladies, so I pursued a few. At that time, I never thought of the mating game in terms of selling, but, in retrospect, it has many similar characteristics. [There may be some confusion as to who is the salesperson and who the eager buyer.] Then, there was my political selling described in an earlier chapter. Finally, even in industrial work, there are occasional sales techniques to be learned.

For example, one of my industrial jobs in New York for a phonograph record manufacturer involved control of electroplating baths where metal plates called "stampers" were electroformed. These stampers were later used to stamp out thousands of records. This was a small specialty manufacturer, but some of their output resulted in substantial sales, e.g. pianist Bela Bartok playing some of his own compositions. Probably their hottest item was a country and western number called "Cool Waters," sung by Red River Dave. I had the pleasure of meeting him many years later at Knott's Berry Farm in California, where he used to sit on his rocker providing nostalgia for tourists.

In the record industry, it is imperative that each record and consequently each record stamper be completely free of flaws which would adversely affect sound fidelity. From a technical point of view, this was a fascinating job and extremely educational. It helped me develop high technical and quality-control skills which paid off handsomely later in my career.

However, while intellectually stimulating, it lacked pizzazz, so only two things about it remain in my memory. The first is that I often worked the evening shift in a shop located at West 54th Street and Eighth Avenue. Across the street was a radio station and recording studio where the young Frank Sinatra frequently sang. When I periodically went outside to take the evening air, I was greeted by the sight and sound of hoards of young girls across the way frenetically shouting "Frankie! Frankie!"

I did not realize it then, but I was witnessing a masterful display of promotional selling. Those girls were not there by accident; they were a bridge to sales. Sinatra's publicity people had done their job well. The picture still sticks with me. I have never marketed a product as salesworthy as Frankie, but **the marketing techniques are the same whether it be singers or soap or Selectron.**

The second lingering thought is that it was this job that enabled me to publish my first technical article. It was entitled "Electroplating in the Phonograph Record Industry" and appeared in an industrial journal called Metal Finishing. It was the first of many such articles and subsequently books. In this Publish-or-Perish world, it helped establish my reputation in the metal finishing field, enabled me to get better future positions and polished the writing skills, which I hope are exhibited here. Believe me, such writing skills are important for sales promotion, and sales promotion is a *sine qua non* for successful selling.

In addition, only those who have seen their literary babies in print can empathize with the boost in ego that such publication brings, the beginning of an addiction that is further enhanced by complimentary comments of friends and associates. This accounts for several published articles that followed, enhancing my reputation as a metal finishing expert and giving me the confidence to then tackle the international scene. Result: an appointment by the Ministry of Defense of the Government of Israel to spend the next three years setting up finishing and plating shops for their air force, navy and commercial airline.

Incidentally, during one hiatus between jobs, I did try to get into the advertising and promotion field. I signed up with a couple of employment agencies seeking a job in industrial advertising. At that time (and to some extent even today), advertising of industrial products was pretty dismal, with advertising agencies following the same formats they used for general advertising. I thought that I could combine my recently acquired writing skills with my engineering background and provide more creative advertising for industrial products.

Unfortunately, there was one barrier to such a career switch. Strange to say, it was salary; my current engineering income was much higher than advertising agencies were willing to pay a young novice advertising writer with no experience in the field. I offered to start at a lower salary, but it did no good. The agencies believed, and rightly so, that I would just work for them for a year or so to get some advertising experience and then go on to greener pastures. If not for that barrier, I might have gotten back into sales at a much earlier period in my life.

A SALESMAN EXPLORES NEW YORK

Before boarding a plane for the Middle East, however, I should like to enlighten my fellow traveling salesmen about some of the joys of exploring New York City. In subsequent chapters, I shall give many of the other major cities of the world similar treatment, but New York is my pride and joy, so I shall start there.

Let us assume that you are a Traveling Salesman attending a Sales Conference in New York City. Lucky you. The question is: Will you spend all your spare time there at the bar and hospitality suites in your hotel, or would you rather explore the city a little in the limited time you have available? You will never see it all, which is why I am limiting most of my suggestions to Manhattan, though Brooklyn has recently undergone a resurgence. You will not even be able to cover the limited itinerary I suggest here, but you should try.

After all, traveling and experiencing are part of the *joie de vivre* in the life of a salesman. Consequently, it is my intention to highlight some of the wonders of New York City as they affect this particular peddler's senses. I have neither the time nor the patience to carry out the detailed checking and rechecking needed to give you precise and accurate travel advice. There are many guidebooks which better serve that purpose. What I offer here comes strictly from memory, which means that you will only read about sights and smells and feelings which were impressive enough to be retained by my aging brain and sufficiently streamlined so that a visiting salesman can include a few during brief stopovers in the Big Apple.

Putting it another way, should you visit the Louvre in Paris, you will find there is more to see there than exists in your imagination or your philosophy. You could easily spend four hours there or four weeks or four months. Or you could make a quick and exciting visit to drink in the magnificence of the Mona Lisa and the Winged Victory and leave the rest for another occasion. You would depart with your imagination and senses exhilarated rather than sated. You will have experienced the quintessential Louvre. So let it be with New York City.

I suggest starting and ending your abbreviated tour with magnificence. When I first started this book, I began with a recommended evening visit to the bar of the Windows on the World on the 107th floor of the now defunct World Trade Center. I suggested picking a clear night and viewing the scene below from several different directions. At this point, words fail me. There were no words to describe this seemingly pristine example of one of the truly great wonders of the modern world. Incidentally, their bar served great drinks, probably the largest collection in New York of malt whiskys, Cognacs and Armagnacs, not to mention spectacular frozen daiquiris for the ladies.

Unfortunately, that building is no longer with us, due to 9/11. Its replacement, the Freedom Tower, is nearly completed and will probably be available about the time this book is published. If so, I highly recommend it as a start to your exploration of New York City. Otherwise, try the Empire State Building. You will find the views spectacular but, believe me, it is not the World Trade Center. Still, it is worth a visit. I recommend going about an hour before dusk and staying until all the lights of the city go on after sundown.

Getting back to the present, for the next morning, I recommend a brief walking tour along a short portion of Fifth Avenue. Start at the Rockefeller Center Promenade, midway between 49th and 50th Streets on the west side of Fifth. The decorations along this walk are changed six times yearly, with the most spectacular ones in the Christmas season and the Easter season. Looking westward, take a broad lens view of the Promenade, its seasonal décor, the range of shops on both sides, golden Prometheus in the background, and the final backdrop of the 30 Rockefeller Plaza skyscraper. Stroll along to its end and look down. If you are lucky enough to be there during winter, you will have the pleasure of viewing young ice skaters of all ages gliding and dancing to lively background music and a Christmas tree to end all Christmas trees just behind Prometheus.

Retrace your steps to Fifth Avenue but, if you have a sweet tooth, an expensive one, pick up a quarter pound of mixed truffles at Teuscher along the way. Then, cross Fifth and go into Saks Fifth Avenue. Shop if you must, but at least explore this prime example of a large New York Department Store—one of five or six of the most popular ones. Continue northward along the east side of Fifth Avenue. Visit Saint Patrick's Cathedral on the next block—a must-see irrespective of your religious affiliation. Keep going north. Gape at as many shop windows as you like.

On the next block, go inside the Trump Tower building. Don't miss exploring its lobby and basement areas—a truly excellent example of modern architectural design. Two blocks further and a few steps eastward is the entrance to F.A.O. Schwartz, probably the world's largest and most magnificent toyshop. You can buy toys from $1.00 to $1,000.00 or more. Or you can buy nothing, but regain free of charge some of the fun of your youth.

Retrace your steps to Fifth Avenue, cross the plaza and explore the Plaza, formerly one of New York's old-world hotels, today partially a hotel and part an upscale condo. A coffee, tea or hot chocolate at the Palm Court in the lobby provides a relaxing end to your quick walking tour.

Museums, Restaurants, Bars, Etc.

As I said before, New York is too much. You will never see all of it in a single visit. You will never see all of it if you live there a lifetime.

So don't even try. Pick a few gems and enjoy. Others may strongly disagree with my selection, but trust me. I am a pretty experienced New York City maven, and I know your time schedule. Keep in mind, however, that much of what I tell you comes from memory; many things may have changed.

Depending on your definition, there are between fifty and one hundred museums in New York City. Not to mention an equal number of private art and craft galleries. Short on time? So are we, so let's skip exact addresses. Your hotel concierge, Google or the yellow pages of the phone book can provide precise locations.

Following are my favorites. The American Museum of Natural History is probably the best of its kind in the world. I particularly suggest the African rooms, the dinosaur exhibition and the mineral and gemstone collection. If your interest is art, the Museum of Modern Art also ranks with the world's best. Alternatively, you may stroll along Madison Avenue (50s through 80s) or along West Broadway in Soho and find small galleries offering enough variety to suit any artistic taste. If you have only one or two hours to spare, I strongly suggest the Frick Collection, both for the quality of art displayed and for the majestic former residence in which it is housed, formerly the home of industrialist, financier and art patron Henry Clay Frick. As an added benefit during the dog days of Summer, the Frick is delightfully cool, particularly its central marble atrium.

Another museum famous for its Summer coolness is the Cloisters in Fort Tyron Park, a little out of the way but well worth the trip. The most scenic way to get there is via Fifth Avenue express bus, which works its way up Riverside Drive. This is probably the most distinctive and unusual museum in New York City. It also features medieval music concerts in its central cloister during Summer weekends. The building itself resembles an ancient monastery, into which have been constructed sections of cloisters from European monasteries, nunneries and churches. The Cloisters is an uptown division of the Metropolitan Museum of Art, which we do not include in our recommendations. The Met is a fabulous museum but, like the Louvre, too massive and all inclusive for short visits by the uninitiated, unless there is a special exhibit which you think is just up your alley.

Restaurants are even more difficult to recommend than museums. New York City is the eating capital of the world. Paris is excellent for French or North African food, but New York provides you with wonderful ethnic food from almost all nations and regions. And there is not just one from each region but usually several restaurants to choose from and often at various price levels. If you know your way around, you can get a complete meal for anywhere from $5.00 to $350.00 and up, but there are high quality restaurants in Greenwich Village, the East Village, Soho, Tribeca and Chinatown, where well prepared food is served at $10.00 to $40.00 per meal, particularly in the East Village. Relatively inexpensive luncheon specials abound all over town, even in some of the top restaurants, so it might pay to make lunch your main meal of the day, perhaps with a prospective customer.

With all this available, all I can suggest are a few favorites of different types and prices:

Steak? Everyone has a number one choice. My preference is Peter Luger, an old standby in Brooklyn, a bit off the beaten path but known to every taxi driver. Great steaks in the very informal atmosphere of an old German brew house. Beer galore. Looking for someplace a little bit less expensive, try Knickerbocker Bar and Grill in Greenwich Village. Their T-bone is top notch.

Lobster? If you like them big (4 to 5 pounds, which can be split for two), the classic place to go is The Palm. Three different locations, but I like the ambiance of the original on Lexington Avenue. Much less costly (but missing The Palm's wonderful onion rings) is Francisco's Centro Vasco or, as an alternative, nearby El Quijote.

Fish and Seafood? Let me give you two Gourmet choices. Top rated but also top price (often well over $100.00 for dinner) is a French sea food restaurant called Le Bernardin, one of only seven restaurants in NYC to achieve a Michelin 3-star rating. [Many New Yorkers consider it the best restaurant in the city.] Equally pricey is an Italian sea food restaurant named Marea, also top quality. Both have much better buys on their luncheon menus. For half the price of either of these, you can get a delicious fish dinner, in an aptly named restaurant called Fish in the Village—unfortunately another line-up-to-enter place.

Deli? No question—the Second Avenue Delicatessen (two places, neither on 2nd Avenue). Try the Matzo ball soup and the stuffed cabbage appetizer. Don't forget the pastrami on rye sandwich. Some friends prefer Katz Delicatessen, still at the same Lower East Side location for the past 50 years.

Brunch? [My favorite meal.] A delightful restaurant serving only breakfast, brunch and lunch is Norma's in Le Parker Méridien hotel. The brunch is unfortunately a la carte and the price a bit high, but the experience is worth it. An alternative, slightly pricey place in the East village is called Prune. Must reserve at Norma's. Wait in a long line at Prune. Want something cheaper, but good, try the set menu at North Square, located on Washington Square Park.

French? The last of the old-world, elegant French restaurants in town is La Grenouille. Top notch but high priced. Equally costly but more 2013ish is Bouley. Even more modern and somewhat less costly is Tocqueville. In both of the last two you can get a much better price break at lunch. Want a noisy brasserie type of French restaurant, try Balthazar, a Brasserie in Soho, or a much quieter place, La Lunchonette in Chelsea.

Italian? Da Umberto, on the West side of Manhattan, is a truly wonderful, very homey Italian Restaurant. Equally good, but somewhat more elegant is Il Cantinori on the East side. Both are on the expensive side. On the other hand, a little uptown underground place called Ci Vediamo provides a much more limited menu, but the food is good and the pastas excellent. And the price, including wine, is normally less than $40.00 per person.

Spanish? New York has plenty of decent, but not spectacular, Spanish restaurants. One of the better ones (actually Spanish/French) is a tiny place called Degustation in the East Village. Two others I like for their casual, but pleasant, service are El Charro and Sevilla, both in the West Village.

English? An interesting place serving good steaks and lobsters is Keens Steak House (formerly Chop House). Hundreds of clay pipes hanging from the ceiling add to the old England atmosphere. Highly recommended: their specialty—Mutton Chop, a rare find in U.S. restaurants, even in New York City.

Chinese? By far the most beautiful Chinese restaurant in New York, featuring great Peking Duck, was Tse Yang in midtown Manhattan. An impressive spot to take your best girl. Unfortunately, it recently closed—apparently a victim of the recession. However, I prefer to wander down to Chinatown, where you have over 100 choices featuring relatively good Chinese food, mostly at moderate prices. The Oriental garden is a very good choice, particularly for seafood or a great Dim Sum lunch. If you are a Peking Duck fan, try the restaurant named for that dish. For a pretty good el-cheapo Shanghai style meal, try Nice Green Bo. Crowded but nice.

Indian? Chinese restaurants are much better in New York than in London. For Indian food, the reverse is true. We have many of them, but there are only a few really superior ones. My favorite in Midtown is Dawat—a real gem. And, for a bargain lunch, the best buy in town. Another good and more elegant choice and fancier is Tamarind, which has two locations. If you are seeking much less expensive fare, you have your choice of over a dozen small Indian restaurants in the East Village, an entire block of them on East 6th Street between 2nd and 1st Avenues, or along Lexington Avenue between 26th and 30th.

Japanese? [Since the Author's wife is Japanese, he has had exposure galore, so this is a somewhat larger section than the other ethnic foods.] Most Americans are unaware of the many types of Japanese cuisine. Consequently, it is difficult to choose without knowing your exposure. When I first settled in New York over sixty years ago, there was only one Japanese restaurant here, Miyako. Now, there are hundreds. For the completely uninitiated, the safest choice is probably teppan yaki (grill). A special type of Japanese grill is robata, grilling over an open flame. Robataya in the East Village would be my first choice. You may sit at a table, but a more showy place would be at a semicircular counter, where two robata chefs squat on a raised platform, using long-handled wooden spades to scoop up the raw materials for your choice from a large selection of fish, sea food, meats, mushrooms and vegetables stacked on a sloping counter located between you and them. When the waiter takes your order, he loudly shouts it out to the chefs, who confirm the order by shouting back. A bit of theater. Intriguing and very tasty.

The best known Japanese "cooking" is not cooking at all; it is sushi whose most popular variety is a chunk of vinegared rice topped with a slice of raw fish. If you are more basic, sashimi is the same variety of raw fish without the rice. Both are accompanied by a soy dipping sauce, to which you add a small dollop of wasabi (Japanese horseradish), the amount dictated by the tolerance of your tongue. Two of the best (and very expensive) sushi restaurants are Sasabune and Soto (which also serves cooked fish). The least expensive reasonably good sushi restaurant is Tomoe Sushi in Greenwich Village, very popular with the college crowd. Unfortunately, you will usually have to stand in a long line before getting in to enjoy your food. Lunch is somewhat less crowded. To avoid both the long line and the extra high prices, try

Hatsuhana in midtown or Hasaki in the East village, both of which serve a variety of Japanese foods, but have quality sushi counters.

One other type of Japanese food worth highlighting is a beef and vegetable hot pot called shabu shabu. The restaurant provides the hot pot over a gas flame accompanied by a large plate of thinly sliced meat, vegetables, mushrooms and noodles, which you dip into the boiling, kelp-flavored water, cooking to anywhere from rare to well done, according to your taste. Two dipping sauces are provided. An East Village restaurant (one of two branches) called Shabu Tatsu, open to the wee hours of the morning, is a good bet at a reasonable price. One other popular type of Japanese cooking is tempura (deep-fried, very lightly breaded seafood and vegetables). This is best served at a tempura bar, where they give you only two or three warm pieces at a time. There used to be a wonderful tempura bar at a restaurant called Inagiku in the Waldorf Astoria, unfortunately long gone. Today, some New York Japanese restaurants serve you tempura at your table in larger number of pieces; the result: they get cold by the time you reach your fourth piece. Two other common examples of Japanese specialty cooking are noodles (Soba or Ramen) and teriyaki (particularly salmon teriyaki). Some restaurants provide a sampling of different cooking styles in what they call a Bento Box.

Eastern European? Several choices, but a serviceable place in the Lower East Side, open all hours and a real bargain, is a Ukranian restaurant called Veselka. They serve delicious hearty soups, each a meal in itself, accompanied by thick-cut challah bread. For my money, some of the tastiest soups in town. There are several low priced **Polish** restaurants in the same area with similar menus.

Note that almost all the suggested restaurants are in Manhattan, because visiting salesmen are undoubtedly limited in time. Should you wish to venture to Brooklyn, in addition to the Peter Luger steak House already mentioned, I recommend The Farm on Adderly, one of many good new restaurants in that Borough. The Bronx has meager pickings of superior restaurants, but Robertos in an Italian district there is an excellent choice.

Bars? New York City was once famous for its three B's—bars, banks and bookstores. The number of bookstores is vastly diminished, but the banks and bars multiply like rabbits. Need a blazing fireplace on a snowy winter night? A Greenwich Village bar with the unusual name of One if by Land, Two if by Sea will supply it. For a bar with a view, I recommend the Top of the Beekman Tower or the Salon de Ning lounge at the rooftop terrace of the Peninsula Hotel, an expensive one with an Asian ambiance. Both have fabulous views—not as grandiose as those from the Empire State building, but with the advantage of a clear view, even on a foggy night.

Looking for a good piano bar? Manhattan has at least a half-dozen of them with names like Don't Tell Mama, Brandys and Uncle Charles. If your tastes go to something a little more seedy or funky, try McSorley's Old Ale House, a student hangout with a lively old-world pub flavor. Another (recently re-opened) student hangout with a long history but a more laid-back ambience is Chumley's, a tavern hidden among the twisted streets of Greenwich Village.

A final culinary note. Is there a single restaurant in New York City that I can recommend for visiting salesmen of all tastes? There is. It is called the Union Square Café, just off Union Square. The food is excellent—a combination of Continental and nouvelle American, with sufficient variety on the menu to suit most of us. The bar is well stocked, and the wine list splendid. Prices are moderate to high— roughly $60. to $85. for a complete dinner with wine. Perhaps most important, the service is about as good as you can get. A bevy of polite, helpful and wonderfully cheerful hosts and hostesses greet your arrival. The bartenders are talkative but interesting. You have no problems catching the eye of your waiter or waitress, who really attends to your needs. Every employee is obviously selected and meticulously trained. They are all young and eager to please, in a sense part of the casual, relaxing ambience of the place. Whatever else you order, try the warm banana tart for desert. Only one major problem: you must book early, since the place is usually crowded. However, if you don't mind dining at the bar (which my wife and I prefer), they can frequently squeeze you in at the last minute. [Obviously, I like this restaurant. Have been going there for over 25 years.]

Grand Finale NYC

Enough of bars and restaurants. Just a few more sightseeing tips. If you want to explore the city without tired feet, grab an upper level seat in a New York Big Apple double-decker tour bus or one of several similar tours. Get off and re-board the next bus as often as you like for the same fare. An even better idea. If visiting during the Summer, take a Circle Line boat trip around Manhattan. You get a completely different view of the city.

End your visit as you started—with magnificence. Drive or taxi, preferably in the evening, to the River Café, just below the far end of the Brooklyn Bridge. This is a spot that, even with recent tour-bus forages into the area, not too many tourists know. This is in spite of the fact that it was beautifully photographed in a movie called Moonstruck. When you exit your car or cab, you will view the entire panorama of lower Manhattan, the most spectacular view of the Big Apple. No need to enter the restaurant to enjoy the view, but you might care to end your sightseeing at their restaurant or bar, both drinking in the spectacle and toasting New York City.

THE POWER OF POSITIVE
PUBLICATIONS

In 1942, I was hired for a two-year spell as an Engineering Consultant for the Ministry of Defense of the Government of Israel. What has that got to do with selling? Nothing. Well sort of. I was only 30 years of age, but was hired by a foreign government to set up electroplating shops and metal finishing research and development laboratories for the Israeli Air Force, the Israeli Navy and for its commercial airline El Al. This, in spite of the fact that, while I had plenty of electroplating experience, I had zero background in aircraft maintenance. Furthermore, I was hired at a substantial salary for someone my age.

How was I able to get this relatively prestigious position with such minimal qualifications? The answer is **Salesmanship**. There were essentially three components to this:

1. Preparing a bang-up resume or Curriculum Vitae;
2. Presenting oneself in a way which makes a maximum positive impression on interviewing personnel; and
3. Having a history of articles and papers published in one's particular discipline. [At the University level, this is known as "Publish or perish."]

The first two points are self-evident and need no discussion. These are standard approaches in any book or article dealing with seeking employment. The third requires major emphasis. **Whatever field or industry you wish to work in, publication of pieces written by you for serious scientific, industrial, commercial or cultural journals will give you a substantial leg-up against others seeking the same position.**

I have previously referred to the important concept of "publish or perish" in the world of academia. What few people realize is that the same principal applies to other fields of endeavor. Perhaps not as strongly as in academia, but certainly enough to make a positive impact.

As noted in a prior chapter, a major part of salesmanship is selling oneself. Believe me, one pertinent published article thrown on the desk of the intended purchaser (or employment interviewer) is worth a thousand words of palaver. Publications with your byline in the respective journals covering your industry or specialty pay off in spades when it comes to picking the right plum of an upwardly mobile position or in making the impression required to close an important sale.

And so it was with the Israeli Air Force and me. I was accepted for a job somewhat beyond my experience largely by being able to sell myself through articles I had published. The articles themselves did not deal directly with plating and finishing in the aircraft field, but they did show that I knew my plating business and was on an upward professional curve. Publish or perish is another wonderful slogan for the aspiring salesman in any specialized area.

I worked for three years in Israel, followed by approximately one year of traveling through Europe on my return trip to the United States. During that time, my selling experiences were essentially nil. I did, however, manage to have published articles on electroplating and metal finishing in Israel, Cyprus, Turkey and various countries in Europe. More fuel for the self-aggrandizing fire of future sales success. In addition, these trips of course added to "the things I have seen and the places I have been." More of that in later chapters.

One article I wrote, based on interviews in Europe, dealt with a highly specialized industrial technique called "brush plating," sometimes known as selective plating and, years later, marketed as electrochemical metallizing. This particular chance contact and the resulting article were to a large degree responsible for the future direction of my professional life. This system—widely used in Europe at that time—later caught on in the United States, to a great extent due to my efforts and promotional writings. I was invited to lecture on the subject before several engineering societies and this, in turn, led to the formation of my very successful business venture—a company known as Selectrons, Ltd. [It also enabled me to earn substantial money so that, after retirement, I had the time and the leisure to write ten books, including this one.]

I formed a partnership with a gentleman named Jesse Lane, and we slowly but surely built a business. Our initial investment was $20,000., of which each of us contributed $1,000. The remaining $18,000. was loaned to the company by Jesse on a no-interest basis. My $1,000. was all I could afford at the time. I had unfortunately (or perhaps fortunately) gone through virtually all my savings while wandering around Europe.

Selectrons Ltd. did not prosper quickly. In fact, after several months, Jesse and I periodically went out for a cup of tea or coffee with one question on our minds, "When do we close up shop?" Or, alternatively, "When do we stop throwing good money after bad?" We had gone through nearly a year in business and spent over $17,000. of our $20,000. boodle before lightning struck. Hamilton Standard, an industrial manufacturer specializing in aircraft propellers, placed a substantial order with us, with continuing orders for our specialized plating solutions. This meant that we had to work 24/7 to keep up with the solution orders, but we were on our way. Or so we thought.

Unfortunately, Mr. Murphy stepped into the picture. Jet engines started to replace propeller-driven aircraft, and the business from our one substantial and really profitable customer diminished and diminished and diminished. Such are the fortunes of war and business.

However, Hamilton Standard had stopped the bleeding. Their orders over the next few months enabled us to recoup our losses and even pay back some of our investment loan. More important was the psychological boost. We knew then what we had only suspected, that we were in a business with a huge industrial sales potential if we worked hard and had a bit of luck.

We worked hard and had a bit of luck. Business grew, and other substantial customers came our way. But it didn't happen overnight. Our potential customers were huge industrial firms or U.S. Government and military agencies. How could a puny operation such as ours (three employees including the principals) make contact with and establish a beachhead with the industrial community who required our products? We didn't have capital for major advertising. We didn't have the people or the money needed for a large scale selling operation using individual salesmen. Nor was our product one which would set industry abuzz. It was a useful and worthwhile product, but not a major development like penicillin, the jet engine or the iPhone. How to make the sale?

The answer was marketing, and initially that area of marketing involving promotion and publicity.

PROMOTION ON A
PIGGY-BANK BUDGET

This chapter is one of a few dealing almost exclusively with the tools in trade of a salesman. As such, it provides a hiatus from the anecdotal trials, tribulations and fun in the life of a salesman. Though not emphasized in **bold type**, its primary interest should be to those readers involved in selling. Others have the option of skipping to the next chapter.

How does a small, underfunded company, just getting started, market its products? Selling requires marketing, but marketing is more than just selling. It is the prelude to selling. It introduces the many steps, which lead to the ultimate sale. Your product may be the best thing to hit the market since pizza, but that will not guarantee sales until potential customers get the message. Repeating an earlier concept, building a better mousetrap is not enough. You must find a way to ensure that the potential customer is aware of your "mousetrap." You must build a bridge between customer's need to use the product and your need to sell it.

My new company tried many marketing techniques. The more used, the greater the likelihood of expanded sales. The following list of approaches, though not all inclusive, provides a good starting point:

Advertising (newspapers, magazines, T.V., radio, etc.)

Direct-mail promotions
Exhibitions and trade shows
Industrial, commercial or trade books
Magazine articles
Papers presented before trade or engineering societies
Publicity releases
Speakers' bureaus
Symposia
Telephone campaigns
Training schools (in house)
Training school (at client's facility)
U.S. Embassies, consulates and trade centers

I eventually used all of the above, since the principles of "reinforcement" and "synergism" dictated that the more marketing techniques you used, the better would be your results. Again, selling is a numbers game. However, cost is also a factor. The economics of small business enterprises dictated the initial choices and direction. Time is money, but money is also time. If we had had a larger capitalization, we probably could have saved several years in our expansion program.

As it was, we had to make do. Regarding telephone promotion, for example, long distance calls at that time were costly, so they were minimized. Most of our initial telephone promotions were limited to the New York City area. If the needs of a good customer required that we visit Philadelphia or Atlanta, however, we would arrange to stay there a day longer or several hours longer than the customer required. We always brought along a telephone list of "local" leads, so that we could hole up in a phone booth and reach these customers without expensive trunk calls. [Long distance calls are cheaper now, but they used to be very expensive.] Incidentally, some railroad stations, local telephone company offices and a few hotels provide roomier and more comfortable phone booths than the normal ones. Believe me, for extensive calling over several hours, it makes all the difference in the world.

Similarly, our ever minimal bank account forced us—at least at the beginning—to concentrate on the least costly marketing techniques. We found paid advertising very expensive and the use of trade shows prohibitive. Bulk mailings were costly, but selected limited mailings to small, well-targeted groups of companies were relatively cheap. Training schools and symposia vary in cost, but tend to fall in the middle price ranges. It was too early to write a book on our product, though that did come later. Similarly, the use of U.S. Government facilities for increasing exports was premature. This too happened later in our development.

The remaining marketing tools suited our budget and perhaps our temperaments—publicity releases, journal articles, papers presented at societies and associations and contact with speaker's bureaus. All this occurred long before e-mail, Facebook and Twitter—modern promotional techniques—became available. These very inexpensive approaches would have made our mouths water, had we even conceived of them. They are great promotional tools now—relatively simple and inexpensive.

Publicity Releases

It is my opinion today—reinforced by over 50 years of selling experience—that sending publicity releases or news releases to magazines, newspapers and trade journals is one of the least expensive and most effective ways of establishing contacts for future sales. The quality of the responses received will vary, but a certain percentage will always result in sales. Of course, the more releases you send out, the larger will be the resulting sales. My recent experiences with Facebook and twitter is much more limited, but releases can be sent via E-mail or, using these media, much more inexpensively, though the mechanism may differ.

As to the types of publicity releases to be sent out, we found that three types work best, with positive results in the following order: (1) releases concerning new promotional literature; (2) releases describing new products and (3) releases describing new applications for your present products. With certain exceptions, small businesses should not waste time and money on news releases dealing with appointments of new managers, unless the appointee is extremely well known in the industry.

Each publicity release should occupy no more than two pages of double-spaced copy. Editors are most likely to accept the one-page release. Three pages or more should be reserved only for major events—very exciting or newsworthy breakthroughs. New Literature releases should be accompanied by a copy of the new piece. All other releases should enclose a glossy photo (usually black and white). The 8" by 10" size is best, though 4" by 5" photos are acceptable if you are trying to cut costs. Each release should include your company's name, address, phone and fax number and e-mail address so that recipients should know where to send their inquiries. Addresses should be coded with a department number to enable you to determine later which publication published the release.

When I first started doing promotional work, I was concerned about which journals I should send releases to and how frequently I should send them. I sincerely believed that the editors would be turned off by receiving material from my company too frequently. Experience solved both problems. I was marketing an industrial product, so I started by making a list of industrial publications in the United States. As my company grew, this was later expanded to include foreign journals. The list included what is known as "horizontal" publications, which cover general industry, e.g. industrial equipment, maintenance, design and metals. Equivalent non-industrial publications would be Time, the New Yorker, Readers' Digest and probably Cosmopolitan. My original list also covered specialized "vertical" journals dealing with specific industries, e.g. aircraft, electronics, marine, printing, petroleum and the like. Typical vertical publications on the cultural scene would be Barons, Gourmet and Tennis Week. Finally, there are official publications of various engineering and scientific societies.

Releases were sent to the attention of the Editor, using his name whenever available. I soon learned that frequent submissions did not antagonize editors, since they needed the material to fill their regularly scheduled sections on New Products and New Literature. I ended up sending out three releases a month, one in each of the aforementioned categories. Releases went out to all the horizontal publications. Specialized vertical journals only received material relating to their specialties.

Publicity releases are often referred to as "News Releases," the implication being that the material sent must be brand new. Worry not about that point. Once you have run out of brand new material, releases can be entitled "New in Australia" for releases sent there, even though the products can be old hat in the United States. Alternatively, the terms "revised," "updated" or "improved" may be added to your headline when sending out slightly dated material.

As my company grew, we found other uses for news releases. In addition to sending them to magazines, we started sending them to our own group of salesmen, managers, distributors and agents to keep them up to date. We encouraged foreign agencies to translate the releases into their own language and to submit them to local journals for publication.

It is important to realize that publicity releases are worthless unless you keep track of the replies and follow through. As soon as a journal publishes one of your items, you should request a "tear sheet" (or, in England, a "cutting") of the page where it was published. Keep a loose-leaf notebook, pasting each tear sheet on a separate page. As returns come in, tote them up on this same page. Send each respondent a letter and product literature. Then, have your sales people "go get 'em."

Magazine Articles

Strange to say, publication of a multi-page article on your product in a commercial, technical or cultural journal will produce far fewer sales leads than a quarter-page news release on the same subject. Nevertheless, such articles or "pieces" are invaluable for marketing. First, they provide respectability ("face") for your product. Second, they provide name recognition—the reader will pay attention when he next sees your add or publicity. Third, the printed article (with expensive typesetting already done at no charge to you) can be cheaply reprinted, providing you with an additional flyer for your customers or potential customers.

For overseas selling activities in countries where English is not the first language, there is an extra plus: the magazine usually has the article translated and then printed in their language at no charge to you. [You would be surprised at how expensive technical translation can be.] You can then have it reproduced. An extra reprint in a foreign language, inexpensively obtained, is very valuable, particularly for a small or new company.

It is flattering to have your own by-line on the magazine article, but greater sales mileage is achievable if you can convince one of your customers to use his name. If you have a customer using your product for an application worth writing about, get his permission (and usually his boss' permission) to have you write up the operation, submit the final copy for his approval and then have it published under his name. Your customer will be pleased and proud to see his name in print, and the journal reader will have much more faith in an article "written by" someone using the product rather than by someone with a financial interest in selling it.

How do you manage to get a piece published in a respectable journal? Sometimes they come to you. You have sent out an interesting news release, and suddenly there is a letter or phone call advising that the Editor is interested in an expanded version. Of course, you accept. In some cases, you are requested to write the article. In others, the

Editor will just solicit additional details, so that a member of his staff can do the piece.

In most cases, however, someone from your company must approach the Editor with the idea for an article. Once you have picked a subject, you have hopefully selected the journal with care. Unlike with New Releases, the rules of the game permit articles to be sent to only one publication at a time. Pick one you believe will create the greatest sales interest in your product, usually a specialized journal for pinpointing an individual application or a horizontal journal for a more general article.

Either write or phone the Editor personally. If you write, either enclose the full article or a one-to-two page summary. If you phone first, and the Editor likes the idea, inquire as to how he or she would like the article slanted, desired length, photos, etc. Once the answer is "yes," don't dally. Get the final version to the Editor in less than thirty days.

It was noted above that the article should be submitted to only one journal at a time. There are exceptions. For example, a piece dealing with electronic controls for aircraft could be sent to both an electronics journal and to an aircraft magazine, but both editors must be so advised in advance. Or the same article can be submitted to different journals in different countries, particularly if the languages are different. When writing or speaking to editors, however, you must be truthful. "This is an exclusive piece for your journal," or "This article is being published in several languages, but is exclusive in Singapore," for example. If the target newspaper or magazine is local, it does no harm to invite the Editor to lunch to explain your article and its value to his or her readers.

Papers for Societies and Associations

Every good salesman with promotional skills keeps a complete list of societies or associations in his territory who might be interested in his product. The salesman may even belong to two or three societies and receive their official publications. Incidentally, these official publications provide another excellent target for articles on your product. The list of societies should be updated annually and should include the name and address of each President and or acting Secretary.

The procedure for placing a paper in a professional society journal is identical to that previously described for trade journals or magazines. Phone or write the Editor, Chief Officer or acting Secretary; send in your paper and follow up by phone regularly to obtain a promised publication date.

Maintaining a Speakers Bureau

This approach can be combined with efforts described in the previous section to get double returns for the same amount of effort. Using a list of Engineering or Professional Societies, twice a year, I would send the head of each society a letter advising that my company maintains a speakers' bureau and offers experienced speakers to address society meetings on the subject of our product and its applications. You can follow a similar procedure. Offer speakers both for local meetings and for national conferences. You will be surprised by the number of requests you get.

Before preparing your talk, discuss which product application would best stimulate the interest of their membership. Find out the time allotted. If sufficient time is available, and if your product lends itself to active demonstrations, offer such a demonstration to reinforce the talk. Of course, check the date, time and place and make sure that required slide projectors, etc. are available.

For annual national conferences, find out if the paper will be reprinted in their journal. If so, make sure you get copies. If the paper will not be printed (and also for local meetings), ask about expected attendance, so you can bring enough photocopies of your paper and other promotional literature to distribute. Make sure you receive a complete list of names and addresses of attendees; this will be helpful for later promotion.

Salesmen who have never been involved with basic marketing will be surprised how successful the above approaches can be. In my case, these techniques enabled a small, new company, undercapitalized and understaffed, to bring its sales up to seven figures quickly and efficiently. In later years, when we started to make money and had available funds for more expensive promotional activities such as paid advertising and trade shows, we expanded our marketing techniques. Details on this will be provided in a later chapter, as will the connections between selling skills and company growth, both domestically and eventually overseas.

Before going into this, however, I will meander a bit on my early experiences combining work, writing, business and travel.

Trade Shows—Large and Small

In the United States, there are hundreds of trade shows every year covering products ranging from Agriculture to Travel and held in States from Alabama to Wyoming. You must realize, however, that when you display your products in such shows, you are competing with the big, big boys. Trade shows are very expensive.

Still, as my little company started to grow, we decided to take our chances, and it worked out well. Getting into a national or international trade show is not difficult; it only takes money. The procedures for setting up your booth are fairly standard. You need lots of signs and photos as background for your equipment display. If possible, you need an attractive young lady as a receptionist to help draw in the crowd. And, if you can actively demonstrate your wonderful product without taking too much time and trouble, an active demonstration attracts a lot more attention than a sterile exhibit. In short, common sense. We did all that successfully at annual electroplating conventions, but we went one better.

Possible buyers come to trade shows to see what's new in their industry. However, they also come to have a good time, to mingle with others in their field. One way of taking advantage of that is to hold a hospitality suite in the hotel adjoining the convention center. Most of the exhibitors do that, but we made our hospitality room special. Almost all served booze and nuts and snacks. My sales nose told me that we could provide a better magnet. The Selectron hospitality suite served good food as well as good wine and liquor. We had ham or roast beef being carved at a counter. Large bowls of shrimp were available, as well as a large bowl of salad. In cities like New York, we served brisket and pastrami sandwiches. In California, Texas or Arizona, Mexican tacos were available. And there was always a large bowl of fresh fruit.

This was expensive but, boy, did it pay off. In electroplating trade shows, our Selectron hospitality room was famous and always crowded. They say that the way to a man's heart is through his stomach. That is also true about the way to a man and his company's wallets.

Mini Trade Shows

One day, my sales nose said to me, "If demonstrations and a little hospitality lead to sales at national trade show, shouldn't that work equally well in the local areas where the potential customer is located?" So, I borrowed a procedure from the clothing industry. For years, whenever a new line of styles came out, they would rent a display room in a hotel in a major city, bring along samples of their latest styles and invite clothing store owners or managers to visit, view and hopefully order. It apparently worked for them, so why not for me?

In a previous chapter, I spoke of keeping records of any potential customers who had requested literature on our products or who had expressed an interest in any manner. These records were sorted out with regard to location. Whenever I had a substantial number of inquiries in or near a city, my company would rent a display room at a hotel or motel in that city for a three-day period and mail invitations to all previously interested parties advising them of the location and dates when we would be giving an illustrated lecture on our products together with a demonstration showing how they could benefit by using our equipment.

The idea was a great success. We would normally get anywhere between 20 and 50 visitors to each mini trade show, and a good percentage of these placed orders. [One major exception was a show in Atlanta, where only one person showed up. There had been an unseasonable snow storm in the city, and the temperature had dropped to Zero. In Quebec City, or even in Chicago, that would have been considered normal and not have caused a ripple, but in Atlanta, it was a disaster. As an added catastrophe, we couldn't get eggs for breakfast because the delivery truck had skidded off the road.] We held about six of these mini trade show every year in different parts of the country.

A FEW LEGAL PITFALLS

This will be a short but important chapter. Whether you are out selling for your own company or as an employee or sales agent for a manufacturer, you will be damned lucky if you don't have a legal problem now and then. Such problems cannot be avoided, but they can be minimized.

First of all, before starting a sales job or before opening a company, find yourself a good lawyer to whom you can turn when problems arise. Lawyers are expensive, but not having one can be much more expensive in the long run. If you are employed, never sign a sales contract or an employment agreement without having your lawyer look it over first. Consult with your attorney if you ever feel that you are not being treated fairly. Do this before getting into an argument with your boss.

If you are starting a business, the need for legal advice becomes even more important. Make sure that you are incorporated or have made other legal arrangements to assure that you personally are not responsible for any losses the company may take over and above your original investment. If you are hiring a salesman or arranging for sales agencies or distributorships, make sure that both you and the other party or parties are in full agreement and that everything has been covered in writing and properly signed.

Should you by any chance get into legal difficulties, try if possible to reach an amicable settlement before going to court, even if you are sure that you have the upper hand legally and even if you lose some money in the compromise. My company was involved in two major lawsuits, one which we won and the other which was essentially a draw. These lawsuits cost us about a million dollars each in legal fees, even though we never lost either case. In complicated lawsuits, it is frequently only the lawyers who come out ahead. Arbitration is often suggested as cheaper and faster than a lawsuit, but our experience was otherwise. It is cheaper and faster, but only if you opponent wants it to be so.

Even if you lose badly, and the amount lost endangers your company, don't despair. A good lawyer can often convince your opponent that forcing you into bankruptcy will net them much less in cash than substantially lowering the amount of the settlement. In a case where we did lose badly, our bankruptcy attorney managed to convince the winners to cut the damages in half. Sounds peculiar, but it is a fact, one of the many reasons that you should establish good personal relations with an attorney as early as possible.

GOING INTERNATIONAL

Based upon our selling skills and a huge amount of hard work, combined with the increase of our capital from profits, my company decided to tackle the worldwide market. We had previously found a Distributor in California and a number of Sales Agents in other areas of the U.S. Building on that over a period of years, we opened a subsidiary factory in England and sales offices in Paris, Singapore, Tokyo, Hong Kong and Florida (to cover Latin America). Where we did not have sales offices, we contracted with local international Representatives to market our system. We were on a roll.

We found that the same promotional and sales approaches described in earlier chapters which had worked well in the United States worked equally well overseas. There were, of course, some variations required due to cultural differences, but not too many. I was CEO of Selectrons, Ltd., but I also acted as International Sales Manager, spending four or five months each year visiting overseas offices and the offices of our local Sales Reps in order to bring them up-to-date on new developments and to check on the success or failure of their sales strategies. It worked out successfully, but nothing ever goes entirely smoothly. We had a great deal to learn about the problems inherent in frequent travel, the difficulties that different languages can create and the peccadilloes to be avoided because of cultural differences. However, we found that selling is selling, no matter where it occurs, whether in Pennsylvania or Alabama or Montana or on foreign shores.

The remaining chapters in this book will deal with my lack of such knowledge and how I overcame that void, both overseas and in multicultural U. S. States as well.

AT HOME IN THE SKIES

Travel, of course, requires transportation. Regional salesmen may cover their territories by car, bus or train, but the national salesman, and particularly the international salesman, depends heavily on air transport. This chapter aims to advise salesmen how to achieve maximum benefits from air travel—maximum comfort, maximum convenience, optimum service and, in some cases, minimum costs. Some of my suggestions are routine, but a few of the tips, based on happy or bitter experience, are unlikely to appear in any of the travel literature or salesmen's handbooks.

Which Airline?

Travel magazines periodically feature polls of their readers indicating which airlines are best. Criteria include service, food and the dependability of schedules, among others. The top of the list for different areas of the world differ somewhat from year to year, but there are usually no major surprises. My list, based strictly on my experience, does not vary widely from that of regular travelers polled by the magazines.

A few generalities. Since most airlines provide you with fairly reasonable air transport, all else being more or less equal, and assuming that there is not a huge difference in price, your first choice should be the airline whose departure and arrival times best suit your schedule, give or take 30 minutes. It goes without saying that direct flights will make better time than one-or-two-stop flights and particularly as compared to those involving a change of aircraft. Figure about 45 to 60 minutes wasted for every stop short of your destination. If you need to change planes, figure at least one hour, and sometimes several hours or even an overnight stay wasted in takeoff, landing and waiting time, plus layover time between flights.

I should also add that choosing the "best" airline depends in part on what aspect of airline service is most important to you individually. In my case, it is food, but this led me to a dilemma. When I was in business, most of the world's airlines were my customers, and I have spent time at numerous maintenance facilities. The quality of airline maintenance is controlled by aircraft manufacturers' maintenance manuals and by Government regulations and should consequently be consistent nationally and internationally. Alas, this is just not true. Virtually all airlines have reasonably serviceable maintenance programs and facilities. They have to if they don't want to invite horrendous lawsuits. But some are a damned sight better run and staffed than others. So what was I to do when Airline A served much better food, while Airline B enjoyed superior maintenance. Believe it or not, as a fatalist gourmet, I would choose A.

Speaking of airline food, most of it is frankly terrible, particularly in Tourist Class, and only a bit better in Business Class. I know I overstate the case, but airline food leaves much to be desired, particularly on domestic flights (that is, if they serve food). There are a few rules which may be helpful. Cold food is almost always superior to warm food, which has been reheated on board. Appetizers are usually superior to main courses. [Unfortunately, this is often also true in many restaurants.] This rule doesn't help you very much in Tourist Class, but is a definite advantage in First Class or Business Class where appetizers are plentiful, and you can sometimes request seconds. Even there, I frequently turn down the main course. If hunger dictates that you must eat, chicken is probably your best bet. While not exactly a delicacy, it is kind of hard for a chef to ruin chicken. My second reluctant choice is pasta, which tends to warm up better than meat or fish. Remember, when you reheat a steak at home, you can get fairly good results, but you usually do it under a grill. On planes, they use microwave, and the culinary results are completely different.

Also, keep in mind that special dishes can sometimes be arranged for you at the time of your reservation or if you phone the airline at least 24 hours in advance. These often include vegetarian food, Kosher food (you don't have to be Jewish) and fruit plates. Some of these meals are tastier than the regular fare. On transcontinental flights, I find fruit plates the best bet. Of course, if you are very finicky and don't mind the extra cost, many gourmet food shops prepare take-out meals for airline travel. Note that the airlines do not give credit or rebates if you bring your own meal. These days, bringing your own meal may be necessary for flights in the United States, since many airlines no longer serve meals.

With reference to service, some airlines are better on their domestic runs than on their foreign service, or vice versa. For example, I find the service on United Airlines relatively good on their U.S. flights, particularly on transcontinental flights, e.g. New York to Los Angeles. Service on their flights to the Far East, however, leaves something to be desired, perhaps because I keep comparing their service to that of Singapore Airlines and some other Asian carriers.

Bottom line. For long-run domestic flights, I stick with United Airlines (now including Continental) in spite of a few flaws. I have no major problem with American Airlines as a second choice. For short runs, I prefer Jet Blue or American Eagle in the East and Alaskan Airlines in the West. If you sense only faint praise in these choices, it is because many of the international airlines, particularly when flying to the Far East, are so vastly superior.

For international flights, Singapore Airlines is my top pick, in fact almost everybody's top pick, for traveling to the Far East. However, Cathay Pacific, Thai Airways and both Japanese airlines (ANA and

JAL) are no slouches either. For continental Europe, Lufthansa is unquestionably the best. Swiss Air not bad either, though Alitalia probably has the best food. Air france is second. For England, Virgin Atlantic is superior to British Airways. For Australia, by all means Qantas if you want to fly directly. It is such a long, boring *shlepp*, however, that I recommend flying first to Singapore on SIA (passing through one of the world's best airports), stopping over for a day or two and continuing on Qantas. South American airlines have had financial problems lately, so United may well be as good as you can get.

It might be best to comment on airlines to avoid. I have not traveled to Israel recently, but my memories of El Al include too many seats crowded together and poor food. I understand that they have improved lately, and they do have the advantage of having the best security of any airline in the world. As hinted above, most South American airlines are also guilty of overcrowding, without the security compensation. Jat (formerly Yugoslav Airlines) is equally bad in that respect. But my true *bete noir* is Aeroflot, the Russian Airline. Their planes are uncomfortable, their food even worse. And, were I not a gentleman, I would add something about their flight attendants.

Having made my selections, I must add that attention to some of my subsequent comments may prove more advantageous to the traveling salesman than the airlines chosen.

Choosing a Seat

Seat selection is an art, and like most arts, is highly subjective. Do you prefer window or aisle? (Nobody prefers center.) Front or back? Smoking or non-smoking? [Smoking used to be a problem, but today you have no choice.] Are there criteria for seat choices? You bet there are. From a safety point of view, statistical data indicate that, in a crash, rear seats are slightly safer on impact. The flip side of the coin is that it takes much longer to disembark from the rear, and that most crash deaths result from fire and smoke poisoning rather than from the initial impact. Consequently, an even safer precaution is to choose a seat next to an exit door. Note, however, that airlines place restrictions on those seats. Sometimes, they are not assigned in advance, only at the airport. Children and disabled individuals are not permitted; you must be strong enough and agile enough to open emergency exits easily.

Furthermore, since such seats are in frequent demand, early reservations are strongly suggested if they are available. Unfortunately, due to cost pressures, some airlines now charge extra for them. Sadly, many airlines now even charge extra for aisle seats, for window seats and for bulkhead seats. A recent cute little trick is to separate tourist seats into two groups, adding 3 or 4 inches of leg room to what are now known as "premium" or "comfort" economy class and charging extra for that category.

Another consideration is the state of your kidneys and bladder. If you suffer a prostate condition, if you are pregnant or for any other reason need to urinate frequently, definitely choose an aisle seat. In fact, demand one. If none seem to be available, explain your problem to the airline representative at the counter and/or to the Flight Attendant. Give them a reliable reason, and they will normally make every effort to accommodate you. You might plead in quiet tones that you hate to disturb other passengers with frequent requests to get to the aisle. Were I not the soul of honesty, I might suggest cynically that this ploy will work even if you do not have peeing problems but, like me, are addicted to the extra freedom that an aisle seat permits. When I travel with my wife, we frequently reserve aisle seats on opposite sides of the same row.

On the other hand, if you are an inveterate sightseer and don't want to miss the views on takeoff and landing, the window seat is exactly your choice. For most salesmen, who have taken-off and landed hundreds of times, the comforts of an aisle seat takes precedence. Even for jaded flyers, the window seat is still a must when going somewhere special, e.g. flying into Hong Kong or New York at night or flying over the Grand Canyon or the glaciers of Alaska during the day.

Smoking versus non-smoking problems have been solved in the United States and in most other countries by recent travel rules outlawing the practice, regulations blessed by my wife, who gets ill when anywhere near smoke, but with whom many readers may disagree. However, the problem may still persist in a few overseas airlines. For smokers, the answer is simple: get a seat in the smoking section if one exists. For non-smokers, particularly for those with extra sensitive noses, difficulties continue. For example, if the non-smoking area runs to row 21 and smoking starts at row 22, putting a non-smoker in row 19, 20 or 21 is really a farce. You might just as well be in the smoking section. So, if you are an individual deeply troubled or actually made ill by second-hand smoke, insist on a seat at least ten rows away from smoking.

If no such seats are available, if you have a cooperative flight attendant, if the plane is not overcrowded, and if you are persistent, you might even get upgraded to a no-smoking Business Class seat. [Much less likely these days than it used to be.] I must warn you, however, that, if the Business Class or First Class area is smaller than the tourist areas (usually the case), you are much more likely to be fairly close to active smokers. An excellent solution exists in planes with double-decker seating. Upper level seats are almost always reserved for non-smokers. If smoke is really a serious problem, and for some people it is, better arrange for your flight well in advance and make sure you reserve the exact seat you need.

For the cognoscenti, there are still a number of seating opportunities to be sought. For example, sitting two abreast is more comfortable than sitting three abreast or—horrors—sitting four or five abreast. Unfortunately, unlike theaters, where seating charts exist, it is difficult to find such charts for most modern planes. To begin with, different airlines use different seat configurations for the same model aircraft. There used to be printed charts at every airline counter. Computerization has taken its toll. There may or may not be a chart at the counter, but you are on the wrong side of the desk to see it. You can still, however, ask the Reservations Clerk for this information and make your decisions accordingly. Keep in mind that even when the seat arrangement in most rows is 3-4-3, the plain narrows in some sections, and there are rows with only two seats next to each other.

If you have long legs, and legroom is your primary need, and no seats are available next to an exit door, bulkhead seats, i.e. those directly behind separator walls, usually have slightly wider rows. [These are usually assigned to mothers with infants, since they often have wall attachments or shelves for baby bassinets.] Speaking of legroom, if you can manage to get a seat directly behind a main entrance or exit, after take-off, you can prop your brief case on its edge a foot or two in front of you, cover it with an airline blanket folded double, and use it as a leg rest. Combine this with a reclining seat back, and it is almost as good as a bed. Almost.

If there are two of you traveling together, and neither likes a center seat, try using your imagination. The easiest pick is to find a row with only two seats, usually on the left or right side of the plane. If that fails, ask the clerk if the plane is crowded. If not, you may choose to gamble a little by selecting a window seat and an aisle seat in the same row. Chances are that the seat between you will remain empty. If not, you can almost always arrange a swap with the party in the center seat, since very few people will insist on keeping a center seat. If the plane is going to be crowded, try something else. As previously noted, try to get two aisle seats across from each other. You can still chat and, at the same time, not be cramped.

If you can't get the seat you want while making reservations or even while checking in, there may still be hope. While boarding, politely ask the flight attendant if it is possible to change your seat. If it is extremely important to get a change due to bladder problems, for example, ask for the head flight attendant. If at all possible, they will assist you. Sometimes, however, it is more effective just to take your seat, stow your gear, and stand up and look for opportunities.

This only works if the flight is not full and should not be started until about fifteen minutes before departure time. Is there a seat next to the entrance door or at one of the emergency exits? If seated next to three or four people, can you spot a free two-seater? If you're assigned a center seat, can you see an available aisle seat? Watch for all of these.

If an opportunity presents itself, when should you make your move? It depends to some extent on the incoming traffic pattern. Some flights board early, and it is quickly evident that almost all passengers are in their seats well in advance of take-off time. On others, laggards seem to be straggling in even at the last moment. Very polite passengers who follow rules slavishly will wait until the plane has taken off and the seat-belt light has been extinguished before moving. These people are apt to find that more aggressive passengers have already precluded their intended actions. Nice guys finish last. Normally, the best time to switch to a better seat is three to five minutes before anticipated take-off. Someone with proper reservations may still enter and head in your direction. When this happens, you have no choice but to apologize profusely and get back to your original seat. By then, it is probably too late to make another change. Moving too early increases the chance of this happening. Moving too late may result in someone else grabbing the seat you wanted before you do. Timing is very important, but this is not an exact science.

One type of seat change requires additional discussion. i.e. laying claim to a "bed" on long flights. This used to be much easier when flights were not so full, but it is still sometimes possible. The "bed" I refer to consists of four or five seats in a row in the center line of seats, and is only available to the swift, even when the plane is only half full. On such flights, most of the assigned seats are either in the left or right rows to make sure that the plane load is balanced. Consequently, shortly after you board, you will notice many empty seats in the central rows, particularly towards the rear.

Let us assume you are nicely ensconced in an aisle seat on a flight from New York to San Francisco, but you really need to sleep on the flight, since you have a very busy day ahead of you. You look around and see many available seats in the center rows. About ten minutes before flight time, leave some belongings in your assigned seat and move over to one of the empty center rows. Take some books and belongings with you. In addition, see to it that you have obtained one or more pillows and blankets from the Flight Attendant or from the overhead rack. When making your move, do not take the aisle seat in the center section. If you did that, you may find that someone else has moved into the other aisle seat in the same row. Instead, sit in one of the center seats and spread your books and belongings to the adjoining seats on both sides of you, which discourages other squatters. If additional passengers board and advise you that you are in their seats, apologize nicely and move to another empty row if there is one. If not, your original assigned seat is still waiting.

Once the aircraft has taken off, immediately lie down across three or four seats and spread your belongings over the rest. You will of course need to tilt up or remove the arm rests between seats. Do not wait for the seat belt sign to go off. It is very easy to loosen the seat belt a little and still lie down with the seat belt securely fastened. All of these steps announce to other passengers that you have assumed squatters rights to that group of seats. You may feel a little piggish at first, but rest assured that, unless someone on the plane has had those seats assigned to him or her, you have priority. You will probably notice that other passengers are doing the same thing. It is a question of first seated, first served. The flight attendant can of course "evict" you if she has another passenger with special needs, but that rarely happens. So stretch out, head on pillow (I suggest two pillows to avoid the hardness of the arm rest under your head), cover yourself with one or more blankets; get a good night's sleep. The "bed" you have organized is better than any First Class seat you might have purchased. I can only remember one flight with better sleeping accommodations, a bunk bed on the upper deck of a Philippine Airlines flight to Manila. But that required not only a First Class ticket but also a surcharge.

A few comments on the above. Be aware that, on many planes, first rows in all cabins and those seats directly behind the main exits do not have moveable or removable arm rests. Avoid those rows. Also, to assure your continued possession of your "bed," it may be necessary to forego the late snack the airline has prepared for you. If you, as a salesman, travel fatigued the way I used to, it is a small sacrifice indeed for a good night's rest. Incidentally, once your acquisition of the four seats is assured, be sure to transfer your remaining belongings from your previously assigned seat. And while drifting off to sleep, don't forget to think of me and to resolve to tell all your fellow salesmen to buy this book.

As noted above, due to a recession, many things have recently changed with airline travel. There are fewer flights, so those remaining may be more crowded. And some airlines have now added nuisance fees to fatten their profits. As noted above, many U.S. airlines no longer provide free food. Some have added extra baggage charges, and others have started to charge for some of the preferred seats. One good thing has happened. On international flights, you may now be able to purchase "Premium Economy" seating at much less than the cost of Business Class. The food is the same as in Economy Class, but the seats are sometimes designed to be much more comfortable, and always with greater legroom.

Class Consciousness

Tourist (Economy), Premium Economy, Business or First Class? Which shall it be? Of course, the answer is whatever you or your company can afford. When the Concorde used to fly, you could save time. Time is of course money, but how much money? With the exception that you can be the first to disembark, no time is saved flying upscale classes. Tourist seats arrive at your destination the same time as First Class seats. So what do you get for the extra dough you put out? First Class fares for overseas flights run three to four times

Tourist rates, with Business Class prices in between. For the higher price, you get only two substantial benefits—much better food served more graciously and (most important) much more spacious seats. Of course, there is free champagne, wine and after-dinner drinks; no charge for movies; and more elegant silver and table linen. But the dollar value of these is minimal, as compared to the extra cost.

Top executives I know tell me that they have a much more relaxing trip First Class, and that this enables them to have a more productive business day on arrival. In theory, this makes sense. However, over the years, I have traveled all three classes and have not found the difference in my next day productivity that great. It seems to me that individual physiological characteristics play a greater part in productivity than the comfort of a trip, particularly a short trip. I frequently flew from New York to London overnight, arriving in the early morning ready for a day of selling. [Something I can no longer do.] A former President of my company always suffered jet lag and had to get some extra sleep on his arrival before being able to conduct business. On trips to Asia, he required two days to recover. He never went to Australia, but I hesitate to think what a direct flight there would have done to his bodily functions. More on this later.

Of course, First Class is more pleasant, not to mention being a status symbol, but is it really worth the substantially higher price? For those of us who log tens of thousands of miles yearly, the accumulated cost difference comes to a lot of bucks. Would we be willing to ante up that extra outlay if we were paying the fares ourselves and not charging it to the company? I think not. And if we contribute to company profitability by offering the bread of extra discomfort in traveling, will it not in the long run come back to us as cake, as extra individual income?

Concerning food, as previously noted, cold appetizers in First Class bear no resemblance to those in Tourist. A world of difference. Reheated main courses, on the other hand, are not particularly delicious in either class. By taking a little trouble beforehand, one could bring aboard a lunch or dinner basket from places such as Zabar's or Russ and Daughters and eat splendidly at a small fraction of the fare difference. Unlike movie houses these days, the airlines still have no prohibition on bringing your own food aboard.

It is evident by now that I do not believe in paying the substantial premium required for First Class travel. [My wife disagrees with me.] Business Class is more understandable, but only for very long trips, e.g. New York to Europe or particularly to the Far East. This does not mean, however, that I am opposed to First Class travel if one can arrange it on a Tourist fare. How can that be done? Well, there are ways. They are not usually available, but you should learn to take advantage of them when the situation arises. I am talking about "upgrading," i.e. moving a passenger with a Tourist Class ticket into a Business or First Class seat.

This was often done with members of frequent flyer organizations such as United's Mileage Plus or American Advantage. Airlines like to provide certain benefits to regular frequent flyers, and upgrading is one of the available perks. Join as many of these clubs as possible and, when traveling on a paid ticket, make sure you show the Airline representative your membership card when you check in. Since the squeaky hinge gets the oil, you should always at this time ask if there are any upgrade seats available. Although upgrading these days is much less likely than it used to be, upgrades may still be possible whenever an airline has overbooked its Tourist Class. If this happens and there are available seats in Business or First Class, the airline may upgrade some of its Tourist Class passengers. They still favor any frequent flying members who may be on that particular flight, particularly those who have bought a full price ticket, and of course the club member who has requested upgrading is more likely to be favored over those who have not asked. So, while waiting for your flight, if you hear your name called, chances are that you have been upgraded. As previously noted, this practice has been on the wane during recent years of airline service declines due to a recession. But it is still worth trying and particularly likely to succeed if the Tourist

Class has been widely overbooked. Having a Premium Economy seat also improves your chances of an upgrade.

Incidentally, airline policy is now only to upgrade club members traveling on a full price paid ticket. However, I have found that they are not always strict in enforcing this rule. Even with a discounted ticket, or even occasionally with a free ticket obtained as a frequent flyer bonus, it is possible (though not likely) to get an upgrade. But only if Tourist Class is overbooked and there are no passengers with priority over you. And only if you have so requested when you checked in.

Though frequent flyer club members may get priority on upgrades, it is sometimes possible to be upgraded even if you are not a member of the airline's club. For example, if you have a Tourist Class ticket and are traveling with your spouse or on the same plane with anyone with a Business or First Class seat, have him ask whether it is possible to have you seated next to him or her. If there are seats available and if you are dealing with a kind-hearted agent at the check-in counter, you may be given what is known as a compassionate upgrade. Traveling alone? Strike up a friendly conversation in the waiting room with someone who looks like a prosperous First Class passenger. If the conversation is going well, and if you have a little chutzpah, suggest that he ask if there is room for you to sit next to him or her. No harm asking, and it occasionally works.

While on this subject, I recall with some amusement a whole series of upgradings I received from Lufthansa before there were frequent flyer clubs. Since I hate hanging around airports, I checked in at the Lufthansa counter for a flight to Düsseldorf only twenty minutes before flight time. This was, even then, dangerously close timing for an international flight. If I had been departing from Germany, it would have been too late to check in. But U.S. airports are more accommodating to somewhat tardy arrivals.

In any case, since I was one of the last to check in, I found that all the Tourist Class seats were taken. There was space in First Class so, to my delight, I received an upgrade. I enjoyed the trip tremendously but, during the flight, I said to myself. "Wait a minute. The Germans are very efficient and very well organized. If they overbooked Tourist Class, it was probably not an accident. They probably always overbook." During the next two years, I needed to take five more trips from New York to one or more cities in Germany. With malice aforethought, I checked in less than thirty minutes before flight time on each trip. This involved a risk since, if there had been no First Class seats available, I might have had to wait for a later flight. It never happened. On each and every occasion, Lufthansa had overbooked, and I was upgraded to First Class. Once, I was a touch early. At that time, they had cardboard seating charts sitting on the desk, and I noted that there were still two Tourist Class seats open. I promptly retreated and went to the bathroom. By the time I returned, those were gone, and I received my by then habitual upgrade to First Class.

Verbum sapientia sat!

Fare Choice

The last time I checked, British Airways' lowest listed fare from New York to London during the month of June was about $1400. in Tourist or Economy Class, $4,700. in Business (Club) Class and $15,000. in First Class. Flying to Singapore from LAX, Singapore Airlines was asking $1,600. in Tourist, $6,500. in Business and $13,000. in First Class. Since airline fare rates change everyday (or at least seem to do so), don't count on these figures when you get ready to book. In any case, the figures are crazy. New York to London is 3,456 flying miles; Los Angeles to Singapore requires 8,762 miles of flying. The flight to Asia is more than two and one-half times farther than that to Europe. Shouldn't fares based on mileage logically bear the same ratio? Nay, not so. The Tourist fares to the two destinations are reasonably close. And the Business Class is somewhat more expensive to Singapore than the London flight. And hear this—First Class rates can be even lower than those to London. Loco!

A few years back, in a movie called Sleepless in Seattle, a young girl was questioned about the fare from Seattle to New York. Her answer was, "Nobody knows. They keep changing every day." The movie was a romantic comedy, and the girl's answer was intended as a joke. But you know, many true words are said in jokes.

The fares quoted above are high or peak-season fares, and naturally rates for flying at other times can be much cheaper. Some airlines work on a three-season basis. Most, however, offer only peak-season and off-peak-season fare differentials. If you can arrange your trips during off-peak periods, you will be surprised at the savings. Check with each airline as to their seasonal divisions, but the following are considered normal off-season periods: Asia: January through March; Australasia: April through August; Europe: November through March; and South America: April through November.

Regardless of the season, the fact is that most passengers do not pay the normal listed fares, nor anywhere near them. Check with five different passengers on any flight, and you are likely to find they paid three or four different fares. One can still find ways of getting to London in the $1,000. range. The listed full-fare rates are charged if you order well in advance. If you wait a few weeks, if planes are not filling up as quickly as hoped, those rates may go down. However, at the last minute, if bookings increase, the prices may go up again. All computer controlled. Check prices for different days of the week; some days are cheaper than others. Fridays and Saturdays tend to be higher outgoing, while Saturdays and Sundays are usually higher on return flights.

Don't depend on internet bookings to give you the best price. Sometimes, you will get lower prices phoning the airline directly, though most airlines now charge $25. extra for phone reservations as compared to internet ones. And don't be bashful about requesting a lower price. If you ask, the agent will sometimes surprise you with suggestions. Unfortunately, while the above tactics are great for tourists, salesmen on a tight schedule may need to go along with standard fares. Believe me, the airlines know this.

There used to be and possibly still on rare occasions may be excursions, off-season discounts, off-peak day discounts, APEX fares, Super Saver fares, senior citizen discounts, standby tickets and three-day weekend and holiday fares. These used to be common; For the most part, they are now gone. Special discounts could at one time be obtained by buying your ticket from charter groups, bucket shops, consolidators or coupon brokers; if available, the savings these days are very much less than they used to be. Lower fares were formerly available using tricks of the trade called hub ticketing, split ticketing and nested ticketing. All gone now. And, if you were flexible and had plenty of time (not usual for a salesman), you could get extremely low Courier rates, now a thing of the past. Believe it or not, at one time, discounts of as much as half the listed rates were available if you knew your way around this very complicated pricing thicket. Confused? So am I.

A few brief definitions and clarifications are in order. APEX fares (Advanced Purchase Excursions) must be bought 14 to 30 days prior to departure and dictate that you spend at least seven days at your destination or, in some cases, stay through a Saturday night. Both are intended for vacationers and deliberately designed to avoid use by commercial travelers. Standby tickets were formerly available, but I am not sure whether they still are. These were quite cheap, but did not guarantee a seat. They necessitated waiting around the airport (often for several hours) and getting a flight only if there was an open seat at flight time. If available, they are usually a good bet off-season, but dangerous during peak travel periods, particularly if you have a critical business appointment or are scheduled to deliver a lecture shortly after arrival.

Charter flights have the disadvantage of having a specific hour on an exact date for both departure and return flights. No changes can be made, and there is no refund for cancellations. Obviously not good for salesmen. Consolidators were high volume discount travel agencies who did so much business they got special discounts from airlines, discounts they were willing to share with you—often

20% to 40%. They are probably no longer available. Bucket shops were overseas discount travel agencies, usually only in major cities. They often worked with smaller, cheaper airlines. Coupon brokers used to wholesale unused frequent flyer award coupons, a practice against airline rules and periodically policed by them. Bucket shops and coupon brokers are probably no longer with us but, even if they were, they involved complications and risks most business travelers would not care to take. Consolidators can still be very helpful if you can find one. [Large corporations with many salesmen and executives can still get travel discounts because of the volume of their purchases. They are essentially consolidators.] As previously noted, many former subterfuges have disappeared or are disappearing.

Hub, split and nested ticketing are clever angles some flyers used to reduce rates. For some arcane reason, it may prove cheaper on some airlines to fly to their hub city (the city where their central office and maintenance depot are based), change planes, and continue to your ultimate destination, as compared to flying directly. If a given route is served by only one airline, lack of competition may result in a high price for that flight. You can sometimes get around this by split ticketing, i.e. buying a ticket from another airline, to an intermediate or slightly off-route city, changing planes, and getting a second ticket from that stop to your final destination. While both these techniques may result in cost savings, they do require extra travel time and consequently are usually not available to time-pressed salesman on tight schedules.

Nested ticketing, however, is another story, and is sometimes used by sales travelers for domestic travel. In fact, many large U.S. corporations use this procedure regularly, even though the airlines despise the practice and consider it against airline rules. As previously noted, many promotional or excursion fares give steep discounts over regular fares, but impose conditions such as being away over a Saturday or taking a minimum seven day trip. These rules are deliberately designed to encourage pleasure travel and to prevent business travelers from taking advantage of the lower fares.

However, just as airlines scheme to maintain high fares for business travelers, traveling salesmen (and their counterparts) scheme to get around what they consider unfair rules. Here's how. If you are flying on a Monday from Boston to Dallas, for example, and must return on Friday of that week, just buy two reduced fare tickets. One should show a Monday departure from Boston with a return flight from Dallas on the following Sunday. The second should be a flight ticket originating in Dallas, dated the Friday you wish to return and bearing a return date from Boston a week later. Believe it or not, even if you tear up the return tickets, it is sometimes cheaper to buy these nested tickets than to pay full fare for a short business trip.

A few caveats. Do not order both tickets with a single phone call. The airline may refuse to issue them. In fact, if there are two airlines covering the same route, both with promotional fares, buy each round-trip ticket from a different airline. Make sure the two tickets have different points or origin. If you buy two round trips from Boston to Dallas, planning to use only the stubs you need, it won't work. When the airline computer notices that you did not use the first flight segment, it will cancel your ticket and reservations. You may throw away the unused return tickets. However, if you work for a company with many salesmen, one of your associates may be able to use the other half. Or you can give it as a gift to a friend or even sell it through ads in travel newsletters or by posting a notice on your apartment house bulletin board. The airlines have gotten wise to this, however, and are policing names of flyers much more carefully. On international flights where passports are required, this ploy would be impossible since the names on the return tickets would differ, and there is no way to prevaricate.

Courier tickets are mentioned above, but they are less frequently available, and the cost savings have gone way down. In any case, they were almost never valuable to salesmen and business travelers. A courier is hired, usually on short notice, to pick up an important document or package at the airport and deliver it to someone at the airport destination. Arrangements are made through a courier agency, usually over the phone. Courier tickets used to be free, but too many people offered their services. So the courier agencies imposed a charge, but the cost is no longer as low as it used to be. Unfortunately for business travelers, while there is some flexibility on return flights, departure schedules are rigid and unchangeable. As a salesman, it is unlikely to meet your travel schedules, which are driven by other considerations than cost alone. Courier fares are usually for students, retirees and others with maximum time flexibility. Keep in mind that many things have changed since I was a business traveler.

Finally, a few miscellaneous suggestions. For long domestic flights, e.g. New York to California or vice versa, there are other discount possibilities. Some airlines offer reduced fares on "red-eye" flights, i.e. those taking off and/or landing after dark or in the very early morning. I personally made use of red-eyes whenever possible. They saved me a night's hotel expense; they were usually not crowded, so I was able to stretch out; and they enabled me to arrive in the early morning ready for a day's work. Other salespeople I know, whose metabolisms differ from mine, hate these flights and avoid them like the plague. However, if you are like me, red-eyes may offer lower fare opportunities.

Cross country daytime flights are often heavily booked, so some airlines offer other possible savings. If you are willing to fly from New York to San Francisco, for example, with one or two stops or plane changes along the way, say Chicago or St. Louis, you can often get a cheaper rate than using a non-stop. And, if you plan carefully, you might even do a little selling, either directly or by phone, in these stopover cities. The airlines are fussy about this and require that you catch the next plane available to your next stop or destination, but if you sit down with an airline timetable and do a little planning, you can sometimes circumvent this rule by choosing flights with long wait at intermediate stops or even requiring an overnight layover.

Returning to our comparative fares for New York/London on British Air vs. LAX/Singapore on Singapore Airlines, I expressed amazement that the SIA fares were only a little higher and sometimes even cheaper for traveling two-and-a-half times as far. There are many reasons for this, but the principal one is that Singapore Airlines is famous for regularly discounting fares. All airlines provide discounts, but some known to frequent travelers as "discount airlines" do so on a regular basis. Most of these are smaller airlines, but Cathay Pacific Airways, Olympic Airways, Singapore Airlines and Thai International Airways are reasonably large. Other international discount airlines include Air Europa, Air Jamaica, Icelandair, Malaysian Airlines and Virgin Atlantic. None of these have worldwide coverage, but you can often find one which lands where you want to go. For regularly discounted domestic flights, the larger ones are America West (now part of American Airlines) and Southwest Airlines. Other reasonably dependable smaller domestic carriers are Empire and North American.

My company, in its cash-short early days, took advantage of many of the above approaches. As noted, unfortunately most of these money-savers are no longer available or much diminished. This chapter is already overlong, so space considerations prevent my supplying names and addresses of bucket shops, charter organizations, consolidators, coupon brokers and courier agencies—should they still exist A few of these are available on the internet, in your yellow pages or through your travel agent if you are on friendly terms.

Alternatively, and a better way to get all the details you need, is to subscribe to one or more publications dealing in whole or in part with bargain traveling. These include: Best Fares at (800) 635-3033; Consumer Reports Travel Letter, (800) 234-1970; Frequent Flyer, (800) 323-3537; and Travel Smart, (914) 693-8300. Particularly valuable in my eyes are Business Travelers International, (212) 697-1700 and International Living, (410) 234-0515. Also consult Sunday Travel Sections in major U.S. newspapers.

Even with the help of such publications, for most of you, the intricate maze of competing fares is just too much—too complicated, too time-consuming, too arcane. So, find a good travel agent to sort out everything and get you the best deal possible for any given flight or itinerary. This is easier said than done. If you have the good fortune to know a travel agent personally, team up with him or her. Advise the agent of how frequently you travel, be explicit about your need for cost savings, and give the agent plenty of time to plan each trip. Make sure you promise the agent all of your travel business if he can prove that you are getting the best deals. If you do not know a travel agent, avoid the larger, more impersonal agencies with numerous individual agents. Find a small two-or-three-person agency for whom your frequent travel business will be a substantial asset. Quid pro quo. Cooperate with each other and you will both be winners. If your company insists that you use one of the larger travel agencies, try to deal always with the same individual. Get to meet him or her personally, not just over the phone. Establish a friendship if possible. Believe me, travel agencies, particularly the smaller agencies, are actively seeking someone like you—the commercial traveler who books tens of thousands of miles each year. Find the right one, and the travel agent and his or her agency will bend over backward to keep you happy.

Jet Lag

On long plane trips eastward or westward, everyone suffers from Jet Lag, though in varying degrees. It is unfortunately one of the negatives that being a traveling salesman faces, particularly an international one. Though some bodies recover more quickly than others, it cannot be avoided, but there are a few techniques that ameliorate. Harvard University's web site—healthysleep.med. harvard.edu—provides details. Click on "Getting the sleep you need" and "Overcoming factors that interfere."

To save the reader time, here are a few details. Jet Lag occurs when rapidly flying over quick changes in the light-dark cycle. Your body and its internal clock, accustomed to gradual light changes from morning to day to dusk to night and back to morning, finds it difficult to accommodate these rapid light changes, resulting in excessive sleepiness during the day, fatigue and gastrointestinal problems. These negatives seem to be worse when flying towards the east than when flying westward. Long north-south flights may still be fatiguing, but they do not result in Jet Lag, since the light-dark changes are minimal.

What to do about it? There are technological approaches used by NASA, but these don't do us ordinary people much good. There are medications, which arguably may or may not help. The simplest and best ways involve changing a few of your normal activities. For a few days before an eastward trip, e.g. New York to Paris or Rome, start going to bed earlier and waking up earlier. If you are lucky enough to be able to sleep through the flight, that will at least partially avoid the light changes. Wearing sunglasses during the whole flight and even for several hours after arrival is even better. [Disregard the odd looks that people give you.] Keep all lights in your room dim for an hour or two before retiring. A totally different approach: Taking a morning flight rather than a red-eye can be a big help.

Going westward, e.g. New York to Tokyo or even to Los Angeles, do the reverse; retire later and wake up later. No sunglasses. Expose yourself to as much light as possible after landing or on the following morning. Bottom line: The thing is to acclimate your body gradually, rather than precipitously, to changes between light and darkness.

Whatever the direction of your flight, eat lightly on the day before departure and the day of arrival. Also, avoid highly spiced food on those two days. Your digestive processes are not as efficient when changing time zones or even when changing food or water consumption.

Intriguing People

Airline travel gives one the opportunity of striking up acquaintances or even friendships with interesting and intriguing people. Of course, there are many dull people as well, which is why

I always carry a Kindle or a book or two or retreat into sleep where necessary. However, during my hundreds of thousands of travel miles, I have had the privilege and pleasure of talking for hours to fascinating individuals. A woman who owned several Famous Amos cookie stores in the Far East. A man who was Frank Purdue's primary competitor in the chicken business. The chief curator of a New York museum. A woman who insisted on telling me about a passionate affair she was having with a man 25 years younger. An African man whose father had 22 wives and 76 children, of which 54 had advanced university degrees. A Thai woman doing advance research on tropical diseases. Advertising people. Artists. Politicians. Musicians. Doctors. Lawyers. Alas, no Indian chiefs.

This leads to some interesting opportunities. **Never forget that you are a salesman, and salesmen, like police officers, are always on duty. Should you find yourself seated next to a business executive, engineer, buyer, purchasing agent or for that matter anyone who might possibly prove to be a customer for your product, don't miss this golden opportunity—a captive audience. Get out your card, open your briefcase, hand over some literature. You may be on your way to making an unexpected sale.** I remember a New Yorker cartoon on this subject several years back. It showed two people in adjoining seats, one with a look of horror on his face, the other with a gleeful expression. The latter was pulling papers from his briefcase and saying, "Boy do I have exactly the right insurance policy for you." The cartoon was entitled, "Terror at 1,000 Feet in the Air."

And there are other selling opportunities. Airplanes are happy hunting grounds for the single traveling salesman. For starters, there are neat looking flight attendants—away from home and often with time on their hands during a layover before the next flight. And there are hours and hours of flying time to get through. Strike up a conversation. If the chit-chat is going well, extend an invitation for dinner at your destination. If she is free, give her your card and ask her to call you if she has a layover in your city. Don't let your expectations get too high. Flight attendants get hundreds of calling cards regularly and throw most of them away. Keep that in mind, but also be aware that traveling people often get lonely, and flight attendants do sometimes take you up on your offer and call. This may be a real test on how good a salesman you are.

And what if you have the good luck to find an attractive young lady sitting next to you? I remember a delightful conversation with a Filipina girl on a flight from Tokyo to Honolulu. We ate dinner together, had lots of great conversation, probably too much to drink and loads of laughs. Finally, she fell asleep with her head on my shoulder. I too dozed off, and we spent the night head to head. In the morning, when we disembarked, I expressed my enchantment and told her, "It was a pleasure sleeping with you." She giggled and gave me a good-by kiss on the cheek. We never saw each other again.

FUN WITH FOREIGN LANGUAGES

Languages are fun. Languages can be a nuisance. Languages are practical. And a second or third language can, like a desktop computer or a video of your product line, be an important selling tool to the international salesman. The question is: Are additional languages necessary?

How many languages does an international salesman really need? The only language I speak very well (I hope) is English. I do read (decipher) Spanish and French, but slowly; and I roughly—very roughly—carry on uncomplicated conversations in French, Spanish and German, with a little Hebrew thrown in. When I say "conversations," I refer to mundane subjects such as my job, my health, the time of day, what I did last weekend and the latest scandal in the newspapers. When it comes to politics, philosophy or calisthenics, I bow out. My German is really Yiddish, which I picked up as a child to prevent my parents from speaking behind my back. [I couldn't let them get away with that.] But it works with patient Germans. In addition, I can order food and make simple comments in all of the above languages, plus five or six more.

Is all of this necessary? In a word, "No." Languages—even a smattering—are useful tools for establishing camaraderie with Distributors, Agents and prospective customers. Helpful, yes, but necessary, no. In today's commerce, one can manage with only English throughout most of the business world. A large percentage of businessmen on the international scene speak English. Where they do not, they invariably have an assistant or secretary who will interpret for both parties. In some industries, e.g. aircraft, English is *de rigueur.* In others, such as cosmetics, haute couture and the music and entertainment field, it is amazingly common.

That is not to say that additional languages are not valuable. Foreigners are always pleased when you make an attempt to learn at least a few simple pleasantries in their languages. Just as knowing how to use chop sticks properly in the Far East provides you with "face" and helps establish your international credentials, knowing how to say "thank you" or "good morning" or—most important—the toasting equivalent of "cheers" or "to your health" helps make you one of the international boys and greases the skids for closing that elusive sale. So, for starters, here is a small list of words and phrases an international salesman, or anyone who travels frequently, should add to his vocabulary:

English	**French**	**Spanish**	**Italiaqn**
Thank you.	Merci beaucoup.	Muchas gracias.	Grazie.
You are welcome.	Pas de quoi.	De nada.	Prego.
How is everything?	Ça va?	¿Qué tal?	Come sta?
Please.	S'il vous plait.	Por favor.	Per favore.
Good morning.	Bonjour.	Buenos dias.	Buon giorno.
Good afternoon.	Bonjour.	Buenas tardes.	Buona sera.
Good evening.	Bonsoir.	Buenas noches.	Buona sera.
Excuse me.	Pardon.	Perdon.	Scusa.
Good bye.	Au revoir.	Adios.	Ciao. (informal)
Cheers (Bottoms up.)	Sante.	Salud.	Cin cin.
I love you.	Je t'adore.	Te quiero mucho.	Ti voglio bene

English	German	Japanese	Chinese
Thank you.	Danke schon.	Arigato gozaimasu.	Seah seah.
You are welcome.	Bitte schon.	Do-itashi-mashite.	Pu yong ker chi.
How is everything?	Wie gehtz?	Ogenki desuka?	Ni haw mar?
Please.	Bitte.	Dozo.	Cheeng.
Good morning.	Gut morgen.	Ohio gozaimasu.	Chow arn.
Good afternoon.	Guten tag.	Kon-nichiwa.	Seah woo how.
Good evening.	Guten abend.	Kon-banwa.	Warn arn
Excuse me.	Entschuldigen mir.	Su-imasen.	Tui poo chi.
Good bye.	Auf wieder sehen.	Sayonara.	Chai chean.
Cheers (Bottoms up.)	Prosit.	Kampai.	Karn pei.
I love you.	Ich Liebe dich.	Sukidesu.	Wa ai ni.

Incidentally, when I was young and had just started international travel, there were two expressions whose foreign equivalents I founds the most useful. The first was "I love you." The second was "Where can I find the bathroom?" In a Spanish or Italian restaurant, you can amuse the waiter bv saying *La dolorosa* when asking for the check. In French, it would be *Le douloureux*, instead of *la cuenta* or *l'addition*. It translates as "pain" or "sadness," the equivalent of "the bad news" in colloquial English.

The above, or variations of the above, constitute what I call courtesy discourse. It says to friends, customers and associates, "Sorry, I do not know your language, but I am at least making an effort." Should you decide to make a serious attempt to become multilingual, however, you may wonder which languages would give you the greatest flexibility in social situations. Strange to say, there are three languages with which you could roam over more than over eighty-five percent of the world without difficulties. English is of course *numero uno*. It is the national language of the United States, Canada, Great Britain. Australia, New Zealand, South Africa and Guiana. It is also widely spoken as a second language in all of Scandinavia, the Netherlands, Switzerland, India, Pakistan, Singapore, Hong Kong, Taiwan, Zimbabwe, Zambia,

Kenya, Guyana and Israel, among others. In fact, there are very few major world cities where you cannot manage with English.

Spanish should be your second choice. It is spoken in Spain, all of South America (except Brazil and Guyana), Mexico, Central America, Puerto Rico and parts of North Africa. It is also widely spoken in substantial portions of the United States—Florida, California. Texas, Arizona, New Mexico, Nevada and New York City. [Portuguese, Brazilians and Italians do not speak it but largely understand it.] For your third valuable language, if you have the patience to study the Mandarin dialect of Chinese, you could converse socially with hundreds of millions of people in China and in various other parts of the world. There are quite a number of different Chinese dialects, but Mandarin is probably the most useful, with Cantonese running second. I know, French is a language of great charm (and with a Diplomatic history), and Japanese at present may have greater commercial value, but I still stick to my three choices for social intercourse.

Should a traveling salesman want to invest time and money in learning languages to give himself a commercial advantage over the competition, English and Spanish are still your best bets. However, I might substitute Japanese for Chinese. Japanese is not as widely spoken as Chinese, but in the industrial and commercial world of today, it is possibly a more valuable language. (That may no longer be true five or ten years from now, and it might take you that long to become proficient.) You will find that a very high percentage of Chinese business men, engineers and executives speak English reasonably well. The Japanese less so. They study it in school for many years, but many of them (not all, of course) still have problems. This may sound funny, but Chinese is much closer to English in its grammatical structure. Japanese is radically different.

There is also a cultural reason why Japanese could prove of greater value in selling. During a commercial visit to all non-English-speaking countries throughout the world, if your potential customer does not speak English, he or she will provide you with the courtesy of a translator or interpreter. Should you be in conference with a group of possibly interested buyers, the interpreter will periodically ask the group to stop while he describes to you in English the substance of the last few sentences of the discussion. In this way, you will be able to keep track of the details of the conversation, correct misconceptions and offer your product in its best light. I regret to say that, in my experience, these interruptions do not always occur in Japan. A competent interpreter is usually available. And the conference may start along the same vein described above. Very shortly, however, you will notice that the pauses for translation will become more and more infrequent. After a while, you will no longer be given a detailed blow-by-blow description. Instead, you will be provided with a brief summary every ten or fifteen minutes. Not the same thing. And, strange to say, the same scenario prevails even with a business group of Japanese who do understand English, e.g. in the aircraft industry. At least, this had been my experience.

I have complained about this to my previous Japanese managers on many occasions, but to no avail. And I do not know why. I have been told that this should not occur with an experienced professional interpreter who is familiar with the mechanism of the meeting, but still am not sure. The Japanese are normally the world's most courteous people, but there seems to be something in the Japanese character which makes them extremely rude under these circumstances. This form of discourtesy is not encountered in Chinese speaking nations. So you have another reason why knowledge of Japanese might prove more valuable to the traveling salesman.

LAUGHTER AND LANGUAGE

If you like to laugh—and most salesmen do—even a partial knowledge of other languages will introduce you to the world of confusion that exists among translators. The Italians have an expression, *Traduttore traditore*, which means that a translator is a traitor. Before you finish with this chapter, you will surely realize the validity of that statement.

Much of the fun results from mistranslations due to hidden dangers in translating idioms and colloquial expressions. Since English abounds with words having double meanings, a phenomenal amount of ridiculous sounding double entendre can be found on signs, posters and notices throughout the world. If you know only English, you will still get a laugh out of faulty translations. However, if you also know another language, this will give you insight as to just how the translator became a traitor and add some depth of feeling to your laughter.

Unintentionally amusing signs can be found anywhere in the world, but are particularly common in those countries where English is practically a second language. Israel is a typical example. The vast majority of Israelis speak English with some ease, but often without the subtle knowledge required to translate idioms and colloquial expressions. While working there over 60 years ago, I saw many signs or notices which made me grin, laugh or howl. Here are a few of my favorites:

Outside a doctor's office: Dr. I.S. Cohen, Gynecologist—Women and Other Diseases.

In a dress shop window: Sale Going On. Special Dresses for Streetwalking.

On a butcher shop door: Sol Ben Ami, Butcher—Slaughters Himself Daily at 4:00 P.M.

In a hotel lobby: Visitors Should Complain at the Office Between 9:00 A.M. and 12 Noon.

In a gift shop: Ici, On Parle Francaise; Se Habla Espanole; English Spoken; American Understood.

Don't be too amused at the distinction between "English Spoken" and "American Understood." There are literally thousands of differences between the British English and American tongues, and many can be embarrassing. A faggot in England can mean a meatball. A fag, however, is a first year student at a private school who is required to perform menial tasks for upper classmen. If you hear an Englishman saying, "John Jones was my fag at Eaton," don't jump to the wrong conclusion. And of course there's the old chestnut about the young English lass, an overnight guest at an American home, asking the host's son: "Please knock me up at 8:00A.M." She just wanted to be awakened with a knock on her door.

So you can see that signs are not the only source of linguistic missteps. Friendly conversations among people with different native languages can lead to funny but embarrassing statements. Back in Israel, I particularly remember traveling in a car with two Englishmen, a Welshman, and his Israeli wife whose English left something to be desired. In a teasing manner, we told her we had heard that, prior to her marriage, she used to pick up men and take them home to sleep with her. She strongly wanted to advise us of her virtue in no uncertain terms. She might have necked or petted a little but she had a "limit" beyond which she would not go. That's what she meant to say. Instead, she said, "No, I didn't have to do that kind of thing.

I had a "border." (To our ears: "boarder.") The poor lady could not understand why everyone else in the car couldn't stop laughing.

Similar sounding words such as the above frequently create amusing confusion. Brazil is one of the best countries in the world for fresh fruit. Consequently, the city is full of open air juice bars. On one of my early visits to Rio, I stopped at one of these and ordered pineapple juice, using what I thought was the Portuguese word for pineapple, namely "*avacashi*." My pronunciation (as usual) was apparently not up to par, and the young man behind the counter thought I had said "*avacach*." They do make what they call avocado juice, a mix of avocado, milk and sugar in a blender, and that is what I was served. Unfortunately, I was not paying much attention. I was preoccupied with gazing at the corner and watching all the girls go by. The result was that I picked up my glass without looking and took a big swallow. What a sensation! Think of it as if you were gulping what you thought was milk and finding that someone had substituted wine.

Other language shockers arise from pure coincidence. In Thailand, they tell of a Muslim visitor who spoke no Thai and communicated only in limited English. In a restaurant, he wanted to make sure that the meat dish he was ordering did not contain pork, which is forbidden in his religion. He wanted to order a beef dish, but couldn't remember the word for cow, so he asked the waiter for "moo." The waiter nodded and went to fill his order. When he returned, the Muslim man re-checked. "Moo?" he asked, pointing to his plate. "Moo," replied the waiter. It was not until several days after consuming this dish that the visitor discovered that, in the Thai language, the word for pork is (you guessed it) *moo*.

Signs, however, still provided the majority of my amusing experiences with mixed up translations. Or sometimes just due to unintended word juxtapositions. A chain of restaurant/gas station combinations on certain U.S. highways wanted travelers to fill their gas tanks and their stomachs in a single stop. Their sign read: "Eat Here. Get Gas." Or there may be an intended confusion of ideas.

An overhead sign at a Los Angeles restaurant used to read: "Eddie Roger's Café. Eddie Roger Appearing Nightly at the Cash Register." One in Sausalito advertised: "Lucky Porky Meat Market. Kosher Delicatessen." A nearby antique store featured: "Mediocre Antiques and Magnificent Junk."

Then there are signs which in themselves are not funny, but where some imaginative soul has penned in an added thought, either out of whimsy or irritation. Two great ones come to mind. The first was a British Airways poster in a London train station. It read: "Lunch in London. Dinner in Paris." Beneath this, an obviously abused soul added: "Luggage in Bermuda." While driving through rural Illinois, I noticed a raised sign saying: "Jesus Saves." Some energetic and irreverent individual had taken the trouble to climb the signpost to add: "Moses Invests."

Let me conclude this chapter with a number of other examples of signs and notices, supposedly in English, but with unintended misinterpretations. Some of these, I have seen myself in one or more places around the world. Others have been contributed by friends and international sales associates—directly or indirectly.

In a Japanese hotel room: You are Invited to Take Advantage of the Chambermaids

In a French rooming house bathroom: Please Clean Tub after Washing Landlady

On a Swiss restaurant menu: Our Wines Leave you Nothing to Hope For

In a Zurich hotel: Because of the Impropriety of Entertaining Guests of the Opposite Sex in the Bedroom, it is Suggested that the Lobby be Used for this Purpose

In a Tokyo bar: Special Cocktails for Ladies with Nuts

In a Hong Kong tailor shop window: Ladies May Have a Fit Upstairs

In a Greek tailor shop: Order Your Suit Now. Because is Big Rush, We Will Execute Customers in Strict Rotation.

In a Moscow hotel room: If This is Your First Visit to the USSR, You are Welcome to It

In an airline ticket office: We Take your Bags and Send them in All Directions

At a Bangkok dry cleaner: Drop Your Trousers Here for Best Results

In a Rome laundry: Ladies, Leave Your Clothes Here. Spend the Afternoon Having a Good Time

In a Norwegian cocktail lounge: Ladies Are Requested Not to Have Children in the Bar

In a Paris hotel elevator: Please Leave Your Values at the Front Desk

In a Budapest zoo: Please Do Not Feed the Animals. If You Have any Suitable Food, Give it to the Guard

In a Russian Monastery: You are Welcome to Visit the Cemetery where Famous Russian and Soviet Composers, Artists and Writers are Buried Daily except Thursday

From a Tokyo car rental brochure: When a passenger of foot heave in sight, tootle the horn. Trumpet him melodiously at first, but if he still obstacles your passage, then tootle him with vigor.

And my all-time favorite—

In a Mexican hotel: The Manager Has Personally Passed All the Water Served Here.

CONTINUING ON THE LIGHTER SIDE

Being a traveling salesman can have many disadvantages. If you are married and have children, you can be away from home for extended periods. National salesmen usually make it home for the weekend, but international salesmen may be away for weeks or months at a time. Fatigue can be a worrisome factor and, as previously noted, rapid changes in time zones wreck havoc with some bodies. Frequent lack of sleep is a big negative, as are frequent changes in diets. I have often said that being able to sleep on planes and a cast-iron stomach are two almost *sine qua non's* for the traveling salesman. Some physiques are just not up to it.

On the other hand, if you are single or in an unhappy alliance, a traveling salesman's job offers many social advantages. [A good friend of mine, an airline pilot, tells me that his job was the only thing which kept his marriage going.] You have the advantage of being able to visit hundreds of interesting places at your employer's expense. If you have a good product and are a talented salesman, you can earn a lot more bucks than you could possibly make in an office or factory job. And, a bigee—girls, girls, girls. [For a traveling saleswoman, it is men, men, men.] The possibilities are almost limitless.

Start out with flight attendants, most of whom are women. Their average age doesn't seem to be as young these days as in former years, but you have just had a particularly beautiful or charming one deliver your drink. Chat her up. Find out where she is based and whether she has a layover at the final destination of the plane. If her destination is the same as yours, tell her you will be a stranger in a strange town and are seeking a dinner companion. Who knows where the road will lead you? If she is not available that evening, give her your business card and ask her to call. However, as previously noted, do not be disappointed if you never hear from her. These ladies get dozens of cards. But some do call, and you can take it from there.

Next—secretaries. As a salesman, you will undoubtedly be visiting business offices. Almost all executives and managers have secretaries, and my experience is that most businessmen choose attractive ones. My experience also indicates that many of them, having experienced the scent of prosperity in their bosses, are on the lookout for men with prosperous possibilities. Not to mention that the allure of something different goes both ways. Chat them up. If you are lucky, sometimes, their bosses will make it easier by suggesting that the secretary show you around town. [Careful however, as previously noted, a secretary can often help make the sale—or break it.] This lucky event happened to me in Thailand, and I almost married the girl; the only problem was that, due to strong family ties, she didn't want to leave Thailand. She is now a top-notch business executive in Bangkok. We are still very good friends. My wife loves shopping with her when we visit Bangkok.

Both of the above avenues for meeting women overseas are good but limited. So are the possibilities of meeting girls in bars, restaurants (waitresses) and hotel lobbies (hotel employees and guests)—traditional pick-up procedures at home. Again, your prospects are somewhat better, since you are a seemingly prosperous foreigner—candy to many local women. Of course, it is even easier if you are good looking.

But I had a better idea, which worked very well for me. It may be a bit dated, but I suspect it works as well today as it did in my time. I suggest you try it. Most major overseas cities, regardless of the local language, have an English language newspaper or periodical. This is true of Singapore, Manila, Hong Kong, Taipei, Tokyo, Jakarta, Paris,

Madrid, Rome and of course London, among others. Try placing a small add in one of their personal columns. Typical copy would be:

SEEKING A FRIEND

American businessman visits your city regularly. Would like to meet attractive young woman to act as a companion for sightseeing, dining, and seeing movies and shows whenever I am in town. salesman362@aol.com

If you are not computer savvy, you can substitute a home address or a P.O. Box number. Incidentally, some newspapers these days might reject your ad, mild as it is, as too suggestive. You might substitute the following:

SEEKING A PEN-PAL

American businessman looking for a pen-pal in your city, a place I visit regularly. Once we have corresponded, we could possibly meet for lunch or dinner when I'm in town. salesman362@aol.com

None of the above copy is *de rigueur*. You can substitute your own words, but make sure it is not too suggestive. Nor too long; advertising copy is expensive. You may advertise in one or more journals, depending on your ports of call. Usually, one or two times per journal is sufficient.

Be prepared to be amazed at the number of replies you will receive or at the quality of the responders. Foreign women who read English newspapers are usually intelligent and reasonably well educated. But do not be deceived. Some may just want to widen their field of friends or acquaintance, but the vast majority are really looking for good husbands. I was always honest with these wonderful ladies, and only went searching when I was single, divorced or legally separated. As to my readers, gentlemen, you are on your own. I am not the keeper of your morals or ethics. I guess that all the old jokes about traveling salesmen are still valid.

You will never again have to spend your travel evenings alone in your room. Quite a variety of women are likely to reply. Ages from 17 to 50. Mostly single, but a few divorced. Some with children, usually a single child. Many with good jobs or professions. Christians, Muslims, Buddhists and non-believers. Tall, short, beautiful, plain—the whole mix. You will of course sort out the ones you wish to write to but, as a courtesy, you might send a pleasant thank-you note to the others. After a letter or two, you might want to give phone numbers and similar information. One important tip. When you arrange for a first meeting, it is better to make it for lunch or a drink rather than dinner. If one or both of you are disappointed, it gives each of you an easy more-or-less polite exit. And one more thing. These are respectable girls. Don't rush it. Give them the same treatment you give the girls at home.

Note that the above suggestion is similar to the matching, dating and mate-seeking services now widely advertised on television, e.g. Match.com, e-Harmony and Christian Mingle. That is now. When I first tried this approach many years ago, to the best of my knowledge, there was only one such service, a small firm in Hawaii. Times change. One other way of meeting girls overseas was one not available to me in my distant past—Facebook and Twitter. Most of the Tweeters and Facebook friends in the United States are American or Canadian. Some serious time spent on these media, however, will bring up a number of foreigners, some of whom may live in the cities you visit. A quick way to establish some early contacts.

Two final comments on this Chapter. First, Good Luck! Second, incidentally, I met my second wife this way and have never regretted it.

SITES

I have previously commented on one special advantage the traveling sales occupation has over most others. You have the opportunity to visit foreign and American cities and to view fabulous places, both natural and man-made. For the sake of brevity, I shall primarily focus on foreign cities, although there are a number of intriguing American cities to visit. San Francisco and New Orleans come to mind. Of course, not every salesman takes advantage of this advantage. I have known salesmen who have traveled hundreds of thousands of miles and have only seen airport lounges, hotel rooms and the insides of offices and factories. Not I. Whenever I planned a trip, I always tried to overlap a local holiday or a Sunday (Saturday in Israel and Muslim countries) when I could do the tourist thing. I know—most salesmen do not have the flexibility I had as a business owner. But still, where there's a will . . .

Oh, the places I have been and the things I have seen! I strongly suggest that all traveling salesmen follow my lead. I have visited almost all the major industrial cities in the world, with the exception of Moscow and Berlin. Their names fall trippingly on my tongue— London, Paris, Madrid, Rome, Stockholm, Istanbul, Tel Aviv, Bangkok, Singapore, Hong Kong, Manila, Jakarta, Tokyo, Beijing, Shanghai, Bombay (Mumbai), New Delhi, Rio, Mexico City, Marrakech, Buenos Aires, Bogota, Lima, Valparaiso, to mention a few, [One of my nieces calls me a "place dropper."] I have spent time in over seventy countries and forty-nine of the fifty American states. Everyone asks which state

I missed. With apologies to former President Bill Clinton, it was Arkansas. Fellow salesmen, you don't have to see them all, but catch a dozen or so, and you will have a much better idea of what the world is really like.

I have not been to some of these cities in many years, and I am sure that they have changed. However, in my eyes, *plus ça change, plus ça rest la même chose*. My four favorites are still New York City, Hong Kong, Bangkok and Tel Aviv. Vastly different, but each characterized by tremendous energy and vitality. Paris is probably the most beautiful man-made city in the world. Rio de Janeiro, probably the city with the most natural beauty. Bangkok and Rio offer you some of the world's most beautiful women, Barcelona has some of the world's most distinctive architecture. For an American, strolling around London is like revisiting one's high school history classes. In short, each place has its distinctive characteristics—some bad, some good, but all intriguing. Let us explore a few of them in depth. A good guidebook will give you much more complete information than I can here, but let me provide a few highly subjective highlights:

American Cities

I have already covered New York, so let me shift to my second favorite U.S. city, **San Francisco**, the city of hills. Several cities lay claim to having been built on seven hills. San Francisco leads the list, each hill sector having its own distinct character. When I was younger, "God give me hills to climb and strength for climbing" was a line in one of my favorite poems. I really enjoyed climbing many of San Francisco's hills. In my older years, when "strength for climbing" has declined, my climbing is much more limited, but I still admire the wonderful setting in which this city is placed, and can still enjoy its popular waterfront. For a great view of the city, cross the bridge to Sausalito and gape. Visualizing those hills, I can understand why

San Francisco has a very young and very youthful population, which makes it a very lively place.

Foodwise, it is also a great city. Many visitors settle for the Dungeness crab, shrimp and lobster available along the wharf. Still, wonderful restaurants abound. Want the best Dim Sum in America (and possibly in the world), have lunch at either of the two branches of Yank Sing. Dumplings galore and a variety beyond your imagination. If you favor soufflés, either as a savory or as a desert (or both), don't miss Café Jacqueline. While there, go to the back and see proprietress Jacqueline, in front of a huge stainless steel bowl, beating the Hell out of the eggs, as she has done for many years. For top-notch American fare with a Continental tang, you can't do much better than a long time favorite, Boulevard. A classic. Like a little hustle and bustle, combined with great food, particularly their mussels? Plouf is your goal. Sit at the bar! Just a few of the palate-pleasing restaurants San Francisco has to offer.

New Orleans is a very distinctive U.S. city with French, Spanish and southern history intertwined in its culture and its cuisine. It is a fairly large town, but visitors usually stick to the French Quarter (*Vieux Carre*) and its Dixieland Jazz and Rhythm and Blues reputation. Visiting salesmen will have fun on Basin Street and surrounding areas with the music from numerous jazz clubs filling the streets with joy. On holidays and some weekends, you can view jazz bands marching down the streets. In addition to the music, however, note that New Orleans is a historical city. The architecture is distinctive, and you most certainly must visit one or more historic homes in the district. A visit to the old cemetery is also worthwhile, where you will see vertical tombs, housing several generations of the same family.

If you love to eat, as I do, New Orleans is the town for you. The traditional food is French Creole, and there are many famous restaurants. Probably the oldest and most popular is Antoine's, particularly well known for their Oysters Rockefeller. That, however, is only one of the many delicious items on the menu. Another place,

K Paul, should remind you that Chef Paul, has appeared on many TV programs over the years. If you are prepared to go uptown, a more contemporary version of French Creole cooking is available at Brigtsen's restaurant. [The name is Scandinavian, but the food, to my taste is, the best Creole cooking I have ever had.] For a totally different cuisine, go to the beautiful Garden District and have Sunday Brunch (or any other meal) at the famous Commander's Palace. Unless things have changed, expect colorful balloons at your table during the Brunch hours.

Chicago is the largest "American" city. No, I have not forgotten New York, which is really an international city; Chicago is culturally more American and has all the pluses and minuses that most very large American cities do. Lots to do and see and many good places to eat but, in my prejudiced eyes, it really doesn't compare to New York. A must visit, however, is to the Willis Tower, formerly known as the Sears Tower, the tallest buildings in the United States before the new One World Trade Center (now Freedom Tower) was completed. It goes without saying that the views are spectacular. Visiting some quality museums and a ride along Lakeshore Drive are also recommended. As for food, Tru is a great gourmet restaurant, very expensive and worth every penny, but only if you have a lot of pennies. One with a distinctive ambiance, very popular with Chicagoans, is the Frontera Grill, with a Frenchified Mexican menu.

Most other American cities also have something to offer the visitor but, unfortunately, television and cinema have so homogenized U.S. towns that they at least partially lose their distinctiveness. I recently visited the town of Sydney in southern Ohio. Looking for a place for dinner, I found thirteen restaurants—all chains like McDonald's or Kentucky Fried Chicken or Domino's Pizza.

Cities Overseas

Let us now concentrate on cities which most American traveling salesmen are unlikely to have visited and which should offer them opportunities to explore during international business visits.

Paris When visiting Paris, you don't need me to tell you to visit the Louvre or Musée D'Orsay or stroll along the Champs Élysée or enjoy the fabulous view the Eiffel Tower offers, or catch a show at the famous Folies Bèrger cabaret. That goes without saying or, as the French say, *ça va sans dire*. There are, however, many smaller, less touted museums and art galleries well worth your time. Typical examples are the Musée Jacamevart-André (art in a splendid former mansion), the Rodin Museum (sculpture) and the Cluny Musée (middle ages—the only museum where I ever saw a chastity belt). There are also many specialized museums, e.g. wine, fashion and medical science (e.g. the former home of Louis Pasteur).

Or, you could just walk around town. For totally different reasons, London and Paris are great walking cities. In addition to the Champs-Élysées and similar well-known spots, three Parisian sections (*arrondissemonts*) very worth exploring are the Marais, with its many distinctive small shops; Montparnasse, with its bars and cafes closely associated with French literary and art history and Montmartre, with its famous white domed Basilica and its twisted, steep little streets. Another example of great walking areas in Paris— the open-air markets. Many of these occur at regular intervals on certain boulevards, e.g. on Blvd. Richard Lenoir (near the Bastille) on Thursdays and Sundays. Boy, what a mouth-watering panoply of fresh farm products and other edibles. Another intriguing regular market area, one of the oldest in the city, is on Rue Mouffetard.

There are, of course, restaurants galore. Unlike New York, however, most of the really top-notch places are either French or North African, with a strange paucity of really good bistros featuring specialties from other ethnic areas. Oh, there are plenty of non-French restaurants, but most are Chinese or burger or pizza places, usually western knock-offs. There are of course a few exceptions. However, the top-level French restaurants are really marvelous.

You may want to splurge, and I mean **splurge**, at one of the highly touted Michelin three-star establishments, e.g. Pierre Gagniere, but watch your wallet. There fortunately are numerous really good smaller and lesser-known French restaurants worth exploring. Good examples are Chez Paul (not too far from the Bastille) or the Dome (in Le Marais). Another tip: Try a cold seafood platter at any one of many brasseries in the city. You can't go wrong.

Something important. Most big cities have tourist bureaus very worth visiting before you start to explore. All of them have long lists of places to see. Pick up a list of recommended sites, take it to the counter and say, "I am here for only 2 (or 3 or 5, etc.) days. Could you please advise me of the most important places I should see in the limited time I have?" Bingo!

London is an entirely different scene than Paris. Also very different in feeling than New York, though the plentitude of tall buildings may appear similar. To an American, London is history. As previously noted, walking around London is like revisiting your high-school history classes. The palace, the Changing of the Guard, Hyde Park, the Tower, the crown jewels, London Bridge, Parliament, Big Ben—keep walking. Many great museums including, of course, the British Museum. Book seats for the theater (sorry, in England, "theatre"). London's theater scene is almost second to none. [New York is a tad more diversified.] For a wonderful bird's-eye view of London, take a ride on their super Ferris wheel, the London Eye.

British food was once scoffed at, but has highly improved in recent years, though still not up to the fare in other major European cities. Dine at some great restaurants, some large but mostly small. My favorite is a very small one in the Capital Hotel on Basil Street. Disconcerting—while I have eaten there many times, I can never remember the restaurant's name. Indian restaurants are always good in Britain. [As previously noted, on average, Indian restaurants are superior in London to those in New York, while the reverse is true for Chinese fare.] Or join the ghost of Charles Dickens at any one of a huge number of pubs (good, bad and indifferent) he frequented—the George IV, the Bleeding Heart Taverne, Ye Olde Mitre and Ye Olde Cheshire Cheese (sit in the cellar).

London is great but, if you have the time, drive around the Cotswolds (about two hours drive from London) and end up in Stratford upon Avon. Shakespeare country, well worth an extra day or two. [Maybe you have a business appointment in industrial Birmingham, not too far away.]

Rome A fabulous city. You will certainly want to join the crowd and visit the Colosseum, the Vatican (particularly the Sistine Chapel; plan extra time, since the lines are long—very long), the Spanish steps, the famous Trevi fountain and the Palatine Hill. Saleswomen will certainly want to include the fashion district, as will loving husbands fearing the wrath of their mates if they leave Rome without a fashionable gift. Here's one intriguing site that most tourists miss: the underground catacombs.

Oh, there's more and more to see. In fact, too much. If you have a choice, however, substitute **Florence** for Rome. Much more compact, so it's easier to catch all or most of the things there that delight the eye. Even better, if you have a free week or more, just rent a car and wander from Italian village to village, rarely more than an hour apart, and each with something new to delight you. Not to mention really great Italian food (some of the best in the world) to satisfy your palate. [Friends who have never traveled much often ask me to recommend the best first journey. I always suggest motoring around Italy.]

Amsterdam and Copenhagen There are so many other cities in Europe worth rambling through if your business trip takes you there. These two small gems are very different but very much alike in many ways. Both offer good food. Both provide many canals to tour on or many interesting bridges to cross. Both are perfect for cycling or walking. Copenhagen has the longest pedestrian street in the world. Amsterdam has more great art museums. Copenhagen offers Hans Christian Anderson's world-famous Little Mermaid, Tivoli Gardens and truly wonderful design and architecture. But they are very similar in feeling, in their sense of freedom and in having a vibrant youth culture.

Hong Kong Let's leave Europe and fly to the Far East. Hugely different. Hong Kong is an Asian version of New York. Busy, busy, busy. Twice as many skyscrapers as NYC. Gorgeous views from Victoria Peak, about as great a panorama as you can get. Wonderful hotels. Wondrous shopping establishments. Cruises to neighboring islands. A view of neighboring China from the border. Most important to foodies like me, truly amazing Chinese restaurants. [A good sprinkling of non-Chinese fare but, as previously mentioned, no other large foreign city provides the high-quality variety of ethnic foods at different prices you get in New York.] But, if you are looking for bustle, this is it.

Here again, and in every major town, get thee to the Tourist Office before starting to explore. One other important point. In the Orient, you have a different culture regarding women. American women bristle at this thought but, truth be told, most of the girls here have been brought up with the concept that it is very important to know how to please a man, and I don't mean just sexually. Things are of course changing, but change is slow.

Shanghai Unquestionably the most modern, businesslike, lively city in China. [Hong Kong is of course part of China, but not totally so.] Shanghai has great, modern hotels, fine food and shopping opportunities up the kazoo. For a westerner, a much more pleasant and attractive place than Beijing which, however, has more worthwhile tourist magnets to visit, particularly the Great Wall—not too far away. Westerners will feel very much at home here in Shanghai. It is now a truly international city and represents the China of the future. Scratch the surface, however, and you will discover that basically it is still Oriental, only with a modernistic veneer. This is essentially true of all the westernized cities of Asia.

Tokyo A very big city. A vibrant city. An exuberant city. Very Japanese, but not an international city the way New York and London are. Some beautiful temples and shrines, but kind of weak on museums and shows of international interest. If you want a different type of show, try a Bunraku puppet show or classical Kabuki performance. It is a perfect town for night owls. Neon lights galore. Happy crowds. Loads of small late-night bars, many with female companionship. Note, however, that the *Mama Sans* watch very carefully. If you love views, the Tokyo Tower is worthwhile, but has recently been surpassed by the Sky Tree—taller and more spectacular. Tokyo has a large number of intriguing parks, many with distinctive features. For a worthwhile river-view, take a local commuter boat trip starting near the Tokyo Tower and ending in Asakusa, fairly close to the Sky Tree and its surrounding restaurant and shopping areas.

Just a few notes on intriguing restaurants. For a great shabu shabu dinner, try Zakuro near the American Embassy. The idea of eating eel may disturb you but, believe me, it is very good when properly prepared. [It does not taste like chicken.] This is exactly what they do at an old eel restaurant called Nodaiwa, near the Tokyo Tower. Tempura bars at most hotels are certainly worthwhile. Want some fun coupled with a good meal, try Inakaya, a robata (grill) restaurant in the Roppongi area. Food coupled with a bit of showmanship. The waiters call out your order while they take it. The grill masters, seated on a raised platform covered with basic food ingredients, parrot the waiters as each dish is called out. They then scoop up the food from the counter using a wooden spade, grill it, and return the finished dish to you. And the dishes are great. Incidentally, this is a late-night restaurant, so there is an elaborate ceremonial changing of the guard (waiters and grill masters) at 11:00 P.M. [As previously noted, New

York City now has similar robata restaurants, including a branch of Inakaya.]

If you have the time, however, get out of Tokyo and wander around **Kyoto**, a very modern but ancient city with old temples and shrines, both beautiful and of rich Japanese historical interest. Spend a night in a Ryokan, a real Japanese inn, where you sleep on Tatami mats, relax in a *yukata* (robe) and are served a *kaiseki* dinner of many small but delicious courses by kimono-clad ladies, while you gaze out the window at gorgeous gardens. Be forewarned, it's expensive.

Or take a weekend trip to Hakone. The trip itself is half the fun. You start with a luxurious train ride (about two hours) from Tokyo to the foot of the mountain or hill where Hakone is located. Connect to a zig-zag (switchback) train moving alternately forward and backward up the mountain, followed by a funicular railroad to complete the climb. On one of the way stations, visit a spectacular outdoor sculpture gallery with Mount Fuji as a background. In Hakone, stay at an *onsen* (hot spring) hotel or unexpectedly at a British colonial type hotel. Do a little shopping and return by a different route—a cable car ride across a valley ending up at the shore of a lake, which you cross in a boat to connect with a different train returning to Tokyo.

Singapore To my mind, one of the best-run cities (or countries) in the world. The streets are clean. There are almost no slum areas. Traffic is well controlled. The education system works. The government is stable. So what is wrong with the place? Well, there is an old joke that, if you ask a local how are things in Singapore, he or she will answer, "Fine." "If you drop a gum wrapper on the street, you get a fine. If you have too many children, you get a fine. Cross the street at other than an intersection, you get a fine. Play your radio too loud—well, you get the idea." In short, unlike in New York or Hong Kong, there are too many rules, and they are strictly enforced. Other than that, it's a fine city, but you wouldn't want to live there. At least I wouldn't.

However, for a tourist, or a visiting salesman for a few days, it is great. Very civilized. Good hotels with fine service. Great Chinese and Malaysian restaurants. [Malaysia is a close neighbor, and many Singaporeans are native Malaysians.] And many things to see and do. In fact, one of the best cities in the Orient for a three-or four-day tourist stop. One of the best bird parks in the world. An interesting zoo, with particularly intriguing nocturnal tours. Some of the finest museums in Asia. Ethnic food areas, e.g. one specializing in Indian food, and seaside restaurants with top-notch seafood. Also, one of the safest cities in the world.

Bangkok Thailand is a rapidly growing commercial and industrial country and, if you have a new or improved product to sell, by all means include Bangkok in your business itinerary. If not, if you are anywhere in Asia, sneak away for a weekend in this wonderful city and country. I am unabashedly a fan; Bangkok is one of my favorite cities in the entire world. It has a little bit of everything. Beautiful temples. Beautiful girls. Beautiful tourist sites to visit. The Temple of the Emerald Buddha is a supreme example. The floating market on the river is fun. The massage parlors are among the best in the Orient. The people are extremely friendly and helpful. And the food is as good as it gets—both the local and the international food. [I knew one steak house that served beef from three different sources—America, Australia and Japan.] Note, however, that Bangkok is probably the city with the worst traffic in the world. During busy periods, your taxi will move at a snail's pace. Looking for a record not worth emulating? More babies are born in taxis on the way to hospitals here than anywhere else.

As hinted in the Prologue of this book, Bangkok is probably the *piece de resistance* of sexual titilation and pleasure in Asia. Plenty of competition elsewhere, but Bangkok takes the lead. Visit one of many massage parlors there. You can get a first-class one-hour massage for a very reasonable price or a special two-hour massage at four times that price. I leave it to the reader to figure out the difference. When you enter, you will see, sitting behind a glass window, many attractive young masseuses, each with a card and number hanging around her neck. Take your pick. If you are a happily married and faithful salesman, tell the manager that you only want the one-hour service. He will advise you as to which young lady is the most experienced masseuse. If you are single and really into the sex scene, skip the center of Bangkok and visit the nearby town of Pattaya—less of a tourist area and more thickly populated by sailors from the port.

Rio de Janeiro Enough of Asia. Perhaps your business travels take you to South America. If so, let me recommend RIO as the place to see. I have previously opined that RIO is one of the most naturally beautiful cities in the world, if not the most. It is famous for its gorgeous beaches. Who has not heard of the Girl from Ipanema? Only one of a huge number of beautiful Carioca ladies. RIO is also famous for its Carnival, held just before Lent every year. Nothing short of spectacular, since they start preparing for it a year in advance. And Rio is a great city with more than a thousand restaurants (many of them superb). I still remember a very elegant, expensive, but delicious Portuguese one called Antiquarious. Did I forget to mention colorful Samba shows?

The guidebooks list plenty of places to visit, but I want to concentrate on spectacular sights and unbelievable views, namely Corcovado and Sugarloaf mountain. Ascend to Corcovado on a special tourist train running through the Tijuca National Park rainforest. Gape at the panoramic view below of a unique city. Climb the stairs to the base of the Christ the Redeemer statue for an even better look at RIO, not to mention glancing upward at this awesome sculpture.

Back to town. Next, take a cable car to Urca hill for splendid views of the bay and the beaches. You're not through yet. Take a second cable car from Urca hill to Sugarloaf. Views, views, views! Lots more to see in RIO. Let your guidebook take it from there.

Sydney It's a long, long *shlepp* to get there, but it's worth it. This is a youthful, vibrant and exciting city. A world-famous Opera House with all kinds of performances, operatic and otherwise. Water sports galore. Unexpectedly good shopping. A zoo, where you can see many animals unique to Australia. Even a night zoo where you can view nocturnal species. Quite good restaurants, but the barby on the beach is still the favorite. One worldwide famous restaurant—Tetsuya, a French restaurant with a Japanese chef.

Want to see a tremendous harbor view? Climb the Harbor Bridge. [I didn't, but my wife did, and she tells me it was marvelous.] Best of all, beaches, beaches, beaches. The better ones require a short ferry trip across the bay. Manly Beach (no pun intended) is one of the closer family beaches. The best fish and chips I ever ate, served on newspapers, was in the Manly Beach area. Start walking along the shore to a number of adjoining beaches. Be forewarned that many of them are nude beaches, and I mean nude. Aussies are sun-lovers. It is odd to find so many nude or semi-nude beaches in Australia, which was originally very conservative, while nearby Bali, where the women went topless for hundreds of years, now has strict regulations against public nudity. [Note that most of the people in Bali are of Hindu background, while the controlling Indonesian Government is Islamic.]

If you have time to get out of town, there are great national parks and wine-tasting areas. Best of all, a side-trip to the town of **Cairns** will enable you to take a boat cruise around the Great Barrier Reef. Indescribable, so I won't even try.

As you have no doubt noted, I have always at least partially rated cities on their restaurants and the quality of their cuisine. One thing I did not note is that there are certain dishes available overseas that you would hesitate to eat. I have eaten snake in Hong Kong, iguana in Costa Rica, grasshoppers in honey and crickets in a spicy sauce in Mexico, snails and sea urchins in France and baby eels (which look like spaghetti) in Portugal. I have never (knowingly) eaten worms, but I have drunk Mescal, which has a worm in the bottle. Andrew Zimmern and Anthony Bourdain would be proud of me. Believe me, the foods which we find acceptable are always based on the culture of your country, rather than on logic. Protein is protein.

Cities galore. I could go on and on and on, but this is not a book on sightseeing. I am just touching on a few of the wonderful cities commercial enough to possibly be part of a salesman's travel scope. There are so many others: Jerusalem, Venice, Buenos Aires, Dubrovnik, Taipei, Delhi, Seoul, Mexico City, Vancouver, Valparaiso, Cairo, . . . And, of course, Seattle, (WA), San Antonio (TX) and St. Augustine (FL).

SIGHTS

In addition to the cities, the world has many wonders, which may require that you step out of town. Rather than list them with reference to their geography, let me provide you with a short list of some of the miraculous places I have seen. I doubt if many of you will be lucky enough to duplicate my travelogue, but let this list be your goal. To quote an old proverb, "A man's reach should exceed his grasp, or what's a heaven for?"

Sights to see in the United States are mostly outside our cities. We are blessed with tremendous sights of natural beauty and a few man-made ones. Our National Parks are superb. I particularly recommend Yosemite National Park; Badlands National Park (North Dakota) and all the National Parks in Utah. Add to these Mount Rushmore (South Dakota), Niagara Falls (best seen from the Canadian side) and the Grand Canyon (Arizona). Windows on the World in New York is unfortunately no longer around, but the new Freedom Tower view may replace it in the near future.

Overseas, listing them in no particular order, here goes: the Great Wall of China; the Taj Mahal (India); Victoria Falls (Zambia/Zumbawi); Iguasu Falls (Brazil/Argentina—by far, the most outstanding); Ayers Rock (Australia); the Great Hall of the People (China); the Eiffel Tower in Paris and the Skytree in Tokyo; the Pyramids and the Sphinx (Egypt); the canals of Venice; a camera safari in Kenya; the

Great Barrier Reef (Australia); a Nile boat excursion in Egypt; a boat trip from Vancouver (Canada) to Alaska; a helicopter trip to a glacier in Alaska or to one in southern New Zealand; the Sistine Chapel (Rome) and the "Surface of the Moon" (near La Paz, Bolivia).

A FEW PRECAUTIONS

Cultural differences in different countries can sometimes lead to embarrassing or even dangerous situations, which international salesmen should avoid. [The same can be said (to a more limited degree) for some areas of the United States.] An innocuous motion in one country can be a grievous insult in another. An American thumb up to indicate agreement has an entirely different meaning in Australia, where it is the same as giving one the finger or "flipping the bird" in America. The same misunderstanding occurs when an American thinks he is thumbing a ride. In England, one needs two fingers (the forefinger and the middle finger) to provide the same insult. Make sure, however, that you are showing the back of your hand when you do this. The same gesture showing the front of your hand is Winston Churchill's sign for "Victory."

The "OK" signal, making an "O" with your thumb and forefinger to indicate agreement in the U.S. is an insult in Germany, the equivalent of calling someone an "asshole." One of the worst insults in S.E. Asia, and particularly in Thailand, is to point the soles of your feet or your shoes towards another person. Even in the same country, similar but different gestures can be misinterpreted. An American waving good-by with his arm extended and his wrist flexing says "farewell," a gesture which could mean "No" in many parts of Europe. The same American gesture with the arm extended and waving forward and the wrist stiffly aligned with the arm could indicate "good riddance."

The Italian and Greek good-by gesture of wiggling the fingers inward could be interpreted in the U.S. as "Come here."

Greetings such as handshakes vary considerably all over the world. American handshakes are usually quite firm, European and Asian ones more gentle. The Japanese usually bow instead of shaking hands, though this custom may be slowly changing. There are many variations of bowing as a sign of respect—who bows first, and how deep should the bow be. Bowing in the rest of Asia has now mostly been replaced with a handshake. Warning: In many Arab countries, and particularly in Saudi Arabia, do not extend a handshake to a woman. Touching any woman who is not your wife is deeply frowned upon. Incidentally, the same is true among ultra-orthodox Jewish communities in Williamsburg (Brooklyn) and Kiryas Joel in upstate New York.

Touching people provides another category with widespread taboos and varying rules. In Thailand, for example, never pat the head of a friend's or associate's child. Touching people's head is definitely a no-no. Embracing or hugging is also area of deep diversity. In California, everyone seems to hug everyone else, even at first meetings. In New York, some men hug each other, as do some women. However, men do not normally hug women unless they have known them for some time. In Mexico, Spain and Italy, hugging is very commonplace when people meet.

Body gestures even extend to the way one summons a waiter. In the United States, extending one's arm, with the hand facing out or making a beckoning motion with the hand seems to be the standard. In France, a nod of the head is more common. In parts of Mexico, pursing the lips and making a kissing sound while facing the waiter will bring him or her to your table. I strongly suggest not trying this in other countries.

Getting back to respect, be advised that a calling card in Japan is considered an extension of the rank of the person who gives you the card. He will hold the card in both hands when offering it. You are expected to use both hands in accepting it. Never treat the card casually. Don't fold it or stick it in your breast pocket or use it to clean your nails or your teeth. A revealing story: While in business, I gave one salesman the job of covering Latin America and had cards printed with his title "Latin American Representative." He asked to speak to me about this, and nicely requested that the title be changed to "Vice President of Latin American Sales." Not a small matter. He pointed out that, without this designation, he would not be able to see any ranking officer of a company he might visit. Similarly, I should point out that, as President of my company, when in Japan, I was always met by company Presidents. The Vice President of my firm was only met by Japanese firm Vice Presidents. I know this sounds odd to Americans, but it is very important in speeding up international sales.

So many things to learn and so little time. There are books on this subject, and I strongly suggest that every salesman getting an overseas assignment read one before making your first sales trip. Only a small sample is given here. Let us end this chapter with another important Japanese custom. While waiting for an elevator with Japanese associates, I held them back to allow a number of ladies to enter the elevator first. When we reached our floor, I was politely but firmly told, "Mr. Rubinstein, in Japan, ladies do NOT go first." This sometimes led to amusing circumstances. I was visiting Guam, then a favorite honeymooning spot for Japanese couples. In my hotel, I was going down in an elevator with a couple of honeymooners. When we reached the ground floor, I held back and gestured for the young lady to exit first. She, being Japanese, stood back and waited for me to exit. This Alphonse-and-Gaston situation was then repeated. In the confusion, to everyone's consternation, the elevator went back up.

THE RESURRECTION OF A SALESMAN

The author is 91 years of age. [Or should I say 19 years old—with dyslexia?] It has been more than twenty years since I sold my business and essentially stopped being a traveling salesman. But not entirely. Supposedly, I retired in my 70s after that sale. However, I have always believed, and still believe, that retiring to nothing is just putting yourself in the waiting room for death. If you don't have a hobby or a recreational goal or an alternative part-time business activity or charitable activity to retire to, then don't retire.

In the back of my mind, I had always wanted to be an author. One chapter in this book describes my aptitude for writing for promotional purposes and even success with a couple of pieces in the *New York Times*, the *Japan Times* and the *Village Voice*. In addition, I wrote an engineering book on the products I was selling, a book entitled *Electrochemical Metallizing,* which was later translated into and published in German. During the last twenty years of my "retirement," I have had seven non-technical books published on a variety of subjects—six non-fiction and one novel. This book is the tenth book in my writing "career."

Writing is hard, but getting published and getting your books sold is harder. My two engineering books were published by major publishers. Of the remainder, four were published by small publishers and the rest self-published. Small publishers usually do not have the capital to properly promote one's books. And, of course, self-publishing means that sales are up to you. So, guess what, I am back in the selling game. Using some advertising, Facebook and copious E-mails, I have been working very hard to sell my new products, and with some success. A week from the day I finished this book, I participated in a book signing at the Yacht Club in Annapolis MD, part of a May Day celebration. My most popular book has sold 10,000 copies, nothing as compared to books by Barack Obama or by mystery writers James Patterson and John Grisham, but considered in the trade to be a very respectable sale. Believe me, selling books is harder than selling industrial equipment. I'm still a salesman and a live one.

So, let me end with a little bit of peddling. My latest (and my best I believe) published book prior to this one is entitled *TO THE RAMPARTS! Religion vs. Science—the Battle*. A very serious study going back hundreds of years. The one before that, a funny take on my being a nonagenarian, *Old Age Ain't for Wimps*, should delight other oldsters like me. Need to know more about me and my books, check out my web site, MarvinRubinstein.com.

Have I made a sale?

# # # # # # # # # #

CURRICULUM VITAE OF

MARV RUBINSTEIN

Marv Rubinstein is a nonagenarian who has worked in many professional fields. He studied Chemical Engineering at Cornell University and also has a J.D. degree from Brooklyn Law School.

He has been on the Board of Directors of several companies. For many years, he was Chairman of the Board of a corporation, Selectrons, Ltd. Acting as International Sales Manager, he spent time in 49 states and in over 70 countries. He has lived for extended periods in New York City, Carmel (CA), Puerto Vallarta (Mexico), London, Tel Aviv and Bangkok.

He served as an Adjunct Professor at the Monterey Institute of International Studies in Monterey, California, teaching a course called "Quixotic English" to Translation and Interpretation students. The course covered many of the overlooked English language areas described in his book, the *21st Century American English Compendium*. [A 4th Edition will be coming out soon.]

In addition to two engineering books and eight other books on a variety of subjects (including one on humorous aspects of aging entitled *Old Age Ain't for Wimps)*, Professor Rubinstein has had over 150 papers appearing in technical journals or delivered before professional societies. His articles of a non-technical nature have appeared in the New York Times, the Japan Times and the Village

Voice. For three years each, he published a quarterly newsletter dealing with tea entitled *Tea Timers* and another called *The Affable Curmudgeon*. His latest published book is entitled *TO THE RAMPARTS! Religion vs. Science—the Battle.*

His wife, Chie Hamaguchi Rubinstein, is a certified professional Translator from English to Japanese and Japanese to English. He has three adult children—a son, formerly an Apple Executive VP and currently on the Board of Amazon.com; another son a medical Doctor and Surgeon who also does biomedical engineering research at the University of Washington; and a daughter who writes music and is a professional party organizer.

Professor Rubinstein is a member of the New York Bar and has held membership in several technical societies.